praise for *damn g*

"Stratis shares the secrets that have made hii
unique fillings, this book is the final word or

—Rocco DiSpirito, celebrity chef

"Say *bye bye* to basic dumplings!"

—Foodgod

"The French onion soup dumplings burst with flavor. *Damn Good Dumplings* is such a fab read."

—**Wendy Williams,** TV talk show host

"These dumplings are incomparable. They are to die (or to live) for."

—**Omari Hardwick,** actor

"Stratis hits a home run with his innovative idea of converting traditional sandwiches into dumplings. *Damn Good Dumplings* is a must-read!"

—**Pat LaFrieda,** nationwide meat purveyor

"We love *Damn Good Dumplings* and highly recommend it for every home cook."

—**@Dumplinggang**

what others are saying

"My last meal on earth will be the bacon cheeseburger dumplings at Brooklyn Chop House!"

—**Gayle King,** *O Magazine*

"This is the most innovative idea I've ever seen . . . bacon, cheeseburger and pastrami dumplings!"

—**Rachael Ray**

"These exciting new dumplings will break the internet!"

—**Delish**

"Dumplings should not be this good in a steakhouse, but they are!"

—*Newsweek*

"The Philly cheesesteak and French onion soup dumplings are fantastic!"

—*Forbes* magazine

60
INNOVATIVE
FAVORITES
for
EVERY
OCCASION

damn good
Dumplings

Stratis Morfogen
founder of Brooklyn Chop House and Brooklyn Dumpling Shop
with Jessa Moore & Nicolle Walker

Photography by Alexandra Shytsman

PAGE STREET
PUBLISHING CO.

PAGE STREET
PUBLISHING CO.

First published in 2020 by
Page Street Publishing Co.
27 Congress Street, Suite 105
Salem, MA 01970
www.pagestreetpublishing.com

Distributed by Macmillan, sales in Canada by The Canadian Manda Group.

24   23   22   21   20   1   2   3   4   5

ISBN-13: 978-1-62414-894-1
ISBN-10: 1-62414-894-8

Library of Congress Control Number: 2019940344

Cover and book design by Molly Gillespie for Page Street Publishing Co.
Photography Copyright © 2020 Alexandra Shytsman
Author photo by Daniel Kwak

Printed and bound in the United States

**To my late father, John N. Morfogen,
and author George P. Morfogen
for paving the way for me.**

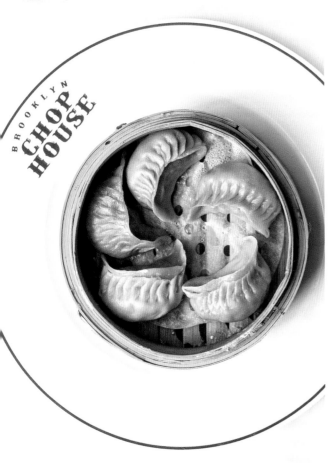

Contents

Introduction

There are two things you should know about me before reading this book.

One: From the time I was four years old, I knew I'd go into the food business. It's in my blood going back three generations.

Two: I never, ever thought I'd end up a specialist, of sorts, in Asian cuisine. That part isn't my blood or birthright—but it's become an essential ingredient in the journey I've taken from being a four-year-old kid washing dishes at the family chop house to today, watching people eat some damn good dumplings.

If you're a foodie, you know every kitchen tells a story. My story starts in the late nineteenth century, with four immigrant brothers who couldn't get a lease. Back in 1896, our familial name was Morfogenis. My grandfather and his three brothers came to America the old-fashioned way, by boat, from a small village in Sparta, Greece, called Anavryti. They left behind their wives and children, like so many other immigrants did, betting that their success in America would open doors to a better life for their children. Instead, the doors to opportunity were slammed in their faces. Anti-immigrant sentiment has always existed in this country, so it shouldn't be a surprise that it took some creative license on the Morfogenis brothers' part to be accepted in the community. They shortened their Greek name to Morfogen and in the blink of an eye, the tides turned. As the Morfogens, my grandfather and great-uncles opened doors to their first business venture, Pappas Restaurant, on the corner of 14th Street and 8th Avenue in Manhattan.

It turned out it did pay to risk it all. From 1896 to 1970, Pappas was regarded as one of the "it" spots in New York City: a see-and-be-seen kind of place for politicians, socialites, celebrities and even presidents.

Bensonhurst, Brooklyn, became my dad's teenage stomping ground. Like many kids of that generation, he started working right away, delivering groceries in the neighborhood and washing dishes at Pappas. With fervent ambition and in the land of opportunity, my father, now John Morfogen, was able to save enough money—twelve thousand dollars, to be exact—to start his own restaurant.

Chelsea Chop House was originally a dilapidated building on 23rd Street and 8th Avenue, just a few blocks away from Pappas. With a decade of experience in the restaurant business under his belt, Dad had the gumption to do what was necessary to succeed and Chelsea Chop House was a smashing success.

By the age of six, I was plating lemon and parsley at Chelsea Chop House. When I wasn't doing that, there were toilets that needed to be cleaned and bathroom floors to be mopped. In some ways, I was like other kids. I complained about these tasks. "I want to learn the business," I'd tell my dad. I often thought I didn't even have to mop the floors at home, so why was I doing it at the restaurant? Dad's answer was simple: "You have to work your way up to become a boss." So, I did.

Chelsea Chop House was open from 1956 until 1985—a 29-year legacy I could not be more proud to claim as my own. My father passed away a few years ago. He was a pillar in his community, a proud businessman, loving father (and grandfather to eleven grandchildren) and a true American success story. I miss him every day, but he is always with me in every business decision and every bite of delicious food we serve. In his honor, I decided to reestablish the name and logo of Chelsea Chop House in my latest venture, Brooklyn Chop House, where our story begins.

By now, I know you're wondering how Chelsea Chop House led to dumplings. Before the mid-1990s, I'd never really explored Asian cuisine; and frankly, my only experience with Chinese food had been in a takeout box. But soon enough, my adventure started to really become "en Vogue"—literally. My wife was an editor at *Vogue* magazine and she often brought me along to dine at events with important fashion industry big shots to places like Mr. Chow, a glitzy hot spot known for its celebrity patrons.

My wife traveled to Paris often as a part of her job and many times I would meet her for weekend getaways. She had always spoken of a little watering hole in the First Arrondissement, named Davé (pronounced da-vé, just like soufflé). The owner was a favorite in the fashion industry and he had Polaroid photos on every inch of his restaurant to prove it. I definitely had to meet him. But more importantly, I had to convince him to come to New York and open his namesake restaurant, where all of the big names would flock, with me as his partner.

During the process, it quickly became clear that Davé was more focused on the celebrity status of the restaurant than the food itself. But, I wondered, in New York City, where a takeout Chinese restaurant existed on every city block, how in the world were we going to pull off a successful restaurant if the focus wasn't on the food? My father had always said, "a good restaurant starts at the source, with every ingredient indispensable to the final culinary experience." I needed to upscale Davé beyond its celebrity hype. I needed to return to my roots and to add the element of value and finesse that my ancestors had always brought to the table. And with my bullish, go-getter demeanor, on my next visit to Mr. Chow, I handed my business card to a waiter asking the head chef to give me a call. The following day, I was in negotiations to bring in Philip Chow, five-star chef of the reputable Mr. Chow for more than 25 years, to become the star of my new Chinese restaurant.

Davé? Well, he kind of fell through the cracks. We renamed Philip "Philippe," to give the name that French flair, and opened the doors to Philippe by Philippe Chow, a four-thousand-square-foot space on 60th Street and Madison Avenue, in December 2005. The rest is history—Philippe quickly became a massive success.

Exploring the novelty and variations of Beijing cuisine was perhaps the most exhilarating culinary experience in my life. Using simple techniques and exotic flavor combinations, a whole new palate opened up to me: sweet, salty, steamed and fried . . . each flavor beautifully complementing the other presented together as one dish. It was so distinct from everything else I had tasted. It was at Philippe that I started my love affair with Beijing food, an affair that has continued all these years.

But the restaurant industry is mercurial, like recipes can be. The perfect balance of ingredients is required to make a recipe as enduring and universal as, say, a diner pastrami sandwich, or the perfect pork dumpling. Sometimes recipes work, and then they don't. After many years of success with Philippe, the flavor turned sour as differences arose between us as partners. We parted ways, and I was on my own for the first time in a decade. It was the perfect opportunity to do some thinking about what was next.

Everything led me to this moment: a combination of destiny and all those choices, good and bad. I decided to fuse my two culinary loves—diner classics and Chinese food—and revolutionize the restaurant industry. They may seem like such disparate worlds, or at least, I thought they might be to the average customer. So, I searched for a common thread. That's where the dumpling came in. Everyone understands what a dumpling is: a bite-sized portion of delicious dough stuffed with assorted fillings. Using the dumpling as my canvas, so to speak, I could both showcase the food I grew up on—corned beef, bacon cheeseburgers, gyros and more—as well as incorporate classic Asian flavors in unique ways to excite the modern palate.

Believe it or not, people loved the marriage of the two cuisines. If you're ever in New York, I hope you'll stop by Brooklyn Chop House, my latest establishment. It's on the Manhattan side of the Brooklyn Bridge, by Nassau Street. Honoring the legacy of my father, this restaurant very much feels like a traditional steakhouse, but the menu is truly creative and unique. Our one-of-a-kind dumplings tie everything together—and keep the customers coming back for more.

I believe this kind of food—elegant but fun, classic yet innovative—should be accessible to everyone. That's where this book comes in. These pages contain the secret to taking the dumpling to the diner level (and vice versa!). With these recipes, you can make these boundary-breaking culinary bites from the comfort of your own home: with your family, to impress friends (or a date!), or just because you're in the mood to try something new. Dumplings are delicious and easy to make and with all my incredible fillings they'll taste brand new every time. This book was decades in the making—I hope you enjoy it. Let's get cooking.

Show Me the Dough

Our Famous "Doughwich" Recipe

YIELD: 72 REGULAR
WONTON WRAPPERS,
36 THICK WONTON WRAPPERS
OR 24 SOUP DUMPLING
WRAPPERS

1 egg

⅓ cup (80 ml) water, plus more if needed

2 cups (250 g) all-purpose flour, plus extra for rolling out dough

½ tsp salt

It's all in the dough. We make our own universal dough in-house, and this can be rolled thinner or thicker, depending on the dumpling filling. A soup dumpling (see the recipes on pages 104–119) needs a thicker wrapper, and so does a hearty sandwich-based filling. You can use premade wonton wrappers for the recipes for this book, but this is an easy recipe for at-home use. (I would also recommend using homemade dough for soup dumplings, as the premade skins are a little too fragile.) Each recipe will specify what thickness of wrapper to use.

This recipe makes up to 72 wrappers, but you can freeze or refrigerate leftovers for later use (see Note). Or, you can have a dumpling party and make several recipes at once. We have dumpling parties with cocktails at the restaurant, and it's a lot of fun. Kids also love to make dumplings, so make it a family project.

In a medium bowl, lightly beat the egg. Add the water and beat until light and foamy, about 2 minutes.

In a separate large bowl, combine the flour and salt. Create a well in the center of the flour mixture in the bowl and slowly pour in the egg and water. Mix well. If the mixture is too dry, increase the amount of water, 1 teaspoon at a time, until a pliable dough has formed. Cover the bowl with a damp cloth and let the dough rest for 10 to 15 minutes on the counter.

On a lightly floured surface, knead the dough until elastic. Cut the dough into two equal balls. Cover the balls with a damp cloth for a minimum of 10 minutes.

To make thin wrappers for minced meat or vegetable filling recipes, cut each ball into four equal pieces. Roll each piece into a 10½-inch (27-cm) square about ⅛ inch (3 mm) thick. Cut each rolled-out square into nine 3½-inch (9-cm) squares. You will have 72 squares.

To make thicker wrappers for sandwich dumplings that have heartier fillings, cut each ball in half. Roll each piece into a 10½-inch (27-cm) square about ¼ inch (6 mm) thick. Cut each rolled-out square into nine 3½-inch (9-cm) squares. You will have 36 squares.

To make thicker wrappers for soup dumplings, cut each ball in half. Roll each piece out until the dough is about ¼ inch (6 mm) thick. Using a cookie cutter, or a drinking glass, cut out circles that are 4 to 5 inches (10 to 13 cm) in diameter. Continue cutting, and re-rolling the dough as necessary, until you have used up all the dough. You will have approximately 24 circles.

Note: You can store extra dough in a plastic baggie in the refrigerator or freezer. It keeps well for 2 weeks in the refrigerator and 1 month in the freezer.

Gluten-Free Wonton Dough

People go gluten free for many reasons—sometimes they can't tolerate wheat or may just want to feel healthier. This dough is completely gluten free and works exactly like the regular wonton dough. We use it in the Vegan Lovers Dumplings (page 103), but anyone who watches their wheat intake can use this dough and substitute it in any recipe.

YIELD: 36 WONTON WRAPPERS

10 oz (285 ml) water

16 oz (454 g) all-purpose gluten-free flour (preferably predominantly rice flour), plus extra for your work surface

1 tsp salt

Bring the water to a boil. In a medium bowl, whisk together the flour and salt. Make a well in the center of the mixture.

Slowly pour half of the boiling water into the well that you created in the flour. Use a fork to incorporate the water into the flour. Continue adding water and stirring until the dough starts clumping together (you may not use all of the water). At this stage, it's time to use your hands.

Sprinkle extra flour onto your work surface. Move the dough to the work surface and start kneading the dough until it becomes one solid ball—it should be firm but not crumbly or sticky.

Knead it on the counter for 2 minutes. Shape the dough back into a ball and wrap it tightly in plastic. Set it aside in a bowl to rest on the counter for 30 minutes to 1 hour.

Cut the ball into four equal pieces. Roll each piece into a 10½-inch (27-cm) square about ⅛ inch (3 mm) thick. Cut each rolled-out square into nine 3½-inch (9-cm) squares. You will have 36 squares.

Note: You can store extra dough in a plastic baggie in the refrigerator or freezer. It keeps well for 2 weeks in the refrigerator and 1 month in the freezer.

Beef
Dumplings

Classic Pastrami Dumplings

YIELD: 24 DUMPLINGS

⅓ lb (150 g) pastrami, finely diced

2 tbsp (6 g) chives, chopped

¼ cup (48 g) sour cream

¼ tsp kosher salt

¼ tsp pepper

⅛ tsp paprika

24 wonton skins, rolled thin

2 tbsp (30 ml) canola or vegetable oil

Spicy mustard, for dipping

The pastrami dumpling is among our most popular treats. It's a little taste of New York City, and surprisingly tasty, even for non-pastrami lovers. The first bite will make you close your eyes and think of Brooklyn. Delicious. Serve with spicy mustard for the full experience.

Fill a small bowl with water. Set aside.

In a medium bowl, combine the pastrami, chives and sour cream until the ingredients are fully incorporated. Season with the salt, pepper and paprika. The mixture will appear gloppy, but the sour cream will absorb into the pastrami and work like glue to hold the filling together as it chills. Place the bowl in the freezer for 15 minutes to let the filling "set."

Lay a wonton dough square on a clean work surface at an angle, so that it looks like a diamond. Place 1 heaping teaspoon of the pastrami filling in the center of the wonton square. Wet your fingers in the small bowl of water and run a damp finger along all four outside edges of the wrapper.

Carefully pick up the wonton skin and lay it in the palm of your hand, keeping the points pointing up toward your middle finger and down to the base of your palm. Gently fold the bottom point of the skin up over the filling, creating a triangle, then gently press the seams to close them well. Using the tip of your finger, wet the two diagonal sides and begin sealing the seam on the left side making small folds from the left side slightly over the right (similar to crimping a pie crust). Remember to line up the edges of the wrapper as you pleat and press all the way around. Continue pleating seven to ten times until the dumpling is completely sealed. The finished dumpling will have a half-moon shape. (See more on page 58.)

Place the finished dumpling on a sheet pan and cover with a tea towel or damp paper towel to keep them moist while working. Continue making dumplings until you have used all the filling and wrappers.

Heat a 12-inch (30-cm) pan with a tight-fitting lid over high heat. Add the oil to the hot pan, tilting the pan until the bottom is covered with the oil. Wait until you see "waves" in the oil, which means it's hot. Place the dumplings, flat side down, in the hot oil about 2 inches (5 cm) apart, making sure the dumplings don't touch. This should be done in batches of eight, to prevent overcrowding in the pan.

Cook the dumplings for 3 to 4 minutes, until they are nicely browned on the bottom. When the dumplings have browned, carefully pour ¼ cup (60 ml) of water into the pan, and put the lid on. Steam for 4 to 5 minutes, until the dumplings are cooked through.

Serve with spicy mustard for dipping.

The Quintessential Reuben Dumplings

Everyone loves a Reuben. It's the classic New York City sandwich, and a good kosher deli is usually where you get this big flavor hit. People travel in for this treat. A Reuben is often a late-night drunk food, and this dumpling is a less messy way to enjoy it. Our homemade Russian dressing adds a zing and cuts through the richness.

Fill a small bowl with water. Set aside.

In a medium bowl, combine the corned beef, Swiss cheese, coleslaw mix, mayonnaise and chili oil until well mixed. Season with the salt and pepper. Place the bowl in the freezer for 15 minutes, to let the filling "set."

To make the Russian dressing dipping sauce, mix the mayonnaise, ketchup and horseradish in a small bowl, and set aside for serving.

Lay a wonton dough square on a clean work surface at an angle, so that it looks like a diamond. Place 1 heaping teaspoon of the filling in the center of the wonton square. Wet your fingers in the small bowl of water and run a damp finger along all four outside edges of the wrapper.

Carefully pick up the wonton skin and lay it in the palm of your hand, keeping the points pointing up toward your middle finger and down to the base of your palm. Gently fold the bottom point of the skin up over the filling, creating a triangle, then gently press the seams to close them well. Using the tip of your finger, wet the two diagonal sides and begin sealing the seam on the left side making small folds from the left side slightly over the right (similar to crimping a pie crust). Remember to line up the edges of the wrapper as you pleat and press all the way around. Continue pleating seven to ten times until the dumpling is completely sealed. The finished dumpling will have a half-moon shape. (See more on page 58.) Place the finished dumpling on a sheet pan and cover with a tea towel or damp paper towel to keep them moist while working. Continue making dumplings until you have used all the filling and wrappers.

Heat a 12-inch (30-cm) pan with a tight-fitting lid over high heat. Add the oil to the hot pan, tilting the pan until the bottom is covered with the oil. Wait until you see "waves" in the oil, which means it's hot. Place the dumplings, flat side down, in the hot oil about 2 inches (5 cm) apart, making sure the dumplings don't touch. This should be done in batches of eight, to prevent overcrowding in the pan.

Cook the dumplings for 3 to 4 minutes, until they are nicely browned on the bottom. When the dumplings have browned, carefully pour ¼ cup (60 ml) of water into the pan, and put the lid on. Steam for 4 to 5 minutes, until the dumplings are cooked through.

Serve immediately with the Russian dressing for dipping.

YIELD: 24 DUMPLINGS

DUMPLINGS

¼ lb (115 g) corned beef, finely diced

⅛ lb (55 g) Swiss cheese (about 3 deli slices), finely diced

¼ cup (18 g) coleslaw mix

¼ cup (55 g) mayonnaise

1 tsp chili oil

¼ tsp salt

¼ tsp pepper

24 wonton skins, rolled thin

2 tbsp (30 ml) canola or vegetable oil

RUSSIAN DRESSING DIPPING SAUCE

1 cup (220 g) mayonnaise

¼ cup (60 ml) ketchup

4 tsp (20 g) horseradish

Bacon Cheeseburger Shumai

YIELD: 24 DUMPLINGS

1 lb (454 g) 80/20 ground beef

2–3 tbsp (30–45 ml) Worcestershire sauce

1 tsp kosher salt

½ tsp black pepper

5 oz (142 g) bacon, cooked crisp and crumbled

24 circular wonton skins, rolled thin

3 oz (85 g) sliced sharp cheddar cheese, cut into small squares

Ketchup, for serving

These are the movie stars of our dim sum menu at Brooklyn Chop House. We go through thousands of these a week, and they have been featured by Gayle King in *O, The Oprah Magazine*. She comes in regularly for them, and we are happy to oblige. These are just as popular with adults as kids—everyone loves a cheeseburger.

Fill a small bowl with water. Set aside.

In a large bowl, combine the ground beef, Worcestershire sauce, salt, pepper and cooked bacon. Mix until well combined.

Place 1 scant tablespoon (12 g) of beef mixture in the center of each wonton skin. Fold the dough up the sides of the beef mixture but don't cover the top. Dip your finger in the small bowl of water. Run your finger along the outer rim of the dough. Carefully fold the dough over itself, similar to crimping a pie crust, to create the classic shumai style.

Place the shumai dumplings in a steamer basket and top each one with a small square of cheddar cheese. Close the steamer basket and place it over a pot of simmering water. Steam for at least 10 minutes (any less time and your shumai will still be partially raw on the inside). Serve immediately with ketchup.

Philadelphia Proud Philly Cheesesteak Dumplings

In Philadelphia, a night out isn't complete without a melty, cheesy sandwich called the "Philly cheesesteak." Chopped steak is grilled to perfection, with melted cheese acting as a stand-in for sauce. It's served "wit" grilled onions. You can also order without cheese—so we made the cheese a dip so you can choose. Of course . . . while it's a preference, you gotta have the sauce.

Place a large sauté pan over medium–high heat and add the butter and 1 tablespoon (15 ml) of the olive oil to the pan. When the butter has melted, add the sliced onions and cook, stirring occasionally, for 15 to 20 minutes, until the onions are soft and brown. Season with 1 teaspoon of the kosher salt and ½ teaspoon of the black pepper. Add the onions to a medium bowl and set aside.

Wipe out the pan and place it back on the stove. Take the frozen rib-eye steak and slice it thinly, then dice it into small pieces. Place the pan back on the stove, over medium–high heat and add 1–2 tablespoons (15–30 ml) of olive oil to the pan. When the oil begins to shimmer, add half of the sliced steak to the pan. Sprinkle with 2 tablespoons (36 g) of salt and 2 tablespoons (14 g) of pepper and let it cook for 4 to 5 minutes on each side, browning well to build the flavor. Add the cooked steak to the bowl with the caramelized onions and repeat with the remaining oil and steak.

Place a wonton wrapper on a clean surface. Place 1 tablespoon (15 g) of the filling in the center of each wrapper. Dip your fingers in the small bowl of water and using a damp finger, wet the outer edges. Bring the left-hand top and bottom points together and squeeze to seal. Bring the right-hand point up to meet the first points and squeeze all the seams tightly to make sure the dumpling is sealed into a 3D triangle shape (see more on page 57). Place the finished dumplings on a sheet pan and cover with a towel. Repeat with the remaining wonton wrappers and filling.

(continued)

YIELD: 24 DUMPLINGS

DUMPLINGS

2 tbsp (28 g) unsalted butter

3–5 tbsp (45–75 ml) olive oil, divided

3 large white onions, sliced into half-moons

1 tsp + 2 tbsp (36 g) kosher salt

½ tsp + 2 tbsp (14 g) black pepper

2½ lbs (1.1 kg) rib-eye steak, frozen for 2 to 3 hours to make slicing easier

24 circular wonton skins, rolled thin

2–3 tbsp (30–45 ml) soybean oil, divided

Philadelphia Proud Philly Cheesesteak Dumplings (cont.)

CHEESE SAUCE

2 tbsp (28 g) unsalted butter

2 tbsp (16 g) all-purpose flour

2 cups (480 ml) whole milk, room temperature

1 cup (130 g) provolone cheese, shredded on a box grater

¼ cup (30 g) grated Parmesan

1 tsp Dijon mustard

1 tsp kosher salt

½ tsp black pepper

Heat a large sauté pan with a tight-fitting lid over medium–high heat. Add 1 tablespoon (15 ml) of the soybean oil to the hot pan, tilting the pan until the bottom is covered with the oil. Wait until you see the oil start to shimmer. Place six to eight wontons in the hot oil and fry for 3 to 4 minutes, until the bottoms are brown and crispy. Carefully pour ¼ cup (60 ml) of water into the pan, and immediately put the lid on. Steam for 2 to 3 minutes, to fully cook the filling and wonton dough. Repeat the process with the remaining wontons.

When cooked, the wonton dough will become soft and pliable, and form to the filling. Serve immediately with the cheese sauce.

To make the cheese sauce, in a small saucepan over medium heat, combine the butter and flour. Cook, stirring occasionally, for 4 to 5 minutes, until the flour is cooked and has started to brown, but be careful to not let the roux get too dark. Slowly whisk in the milk, stirring constantly until the mixture begins to thicken. Lower the heat to low and begin adding the provolone and Parmesan, a handful at a time, while whisking constantly. Make sure all the cheese in the pot is melted before adding the next handful. Whisk in the Dijon mustard, salt and pepper.

Psssst . . . You can also pour the cheese sauce into a bowl and serve warm with crispy wontons.

Short Rib Stacked Dumplings

Short ribs are the richest, stickiest, moistest cut of beef. Braising short ribs makes them incredibly tender. Their hearty richness is great for stews and tacos, and winter is the perfect time to experiment with short ribs in this recipe. We pair these with a really easy and quick pickled onion that has the zing of red wine vinegar and a little sugar. This quick pickle is not only delicious, but it keeps the short ribs from being too rich.

Preheat the oven to 350°F (175°C).

In a small bowl combine the flour, salt, pepper and garlic powder. Lightly coat the short ribs with the flour mixture, then bang off any excess flour (too much flour left on the ribs will make for a gluey finished product). Heat 3 tablespoons (45 ml) of the olive oil in a large, heavy ovenproof pan with a tight-fitting lid (or a Dutch oven). When the oil begins to shimmer, brown the short ribs on all sides until deeply browned, working in batches if necessary. Remove the browned ribs from the pan and set aside.

To the same pan, add the remaining oil, the celery, carrots, onion, garlic, bay leaves and thyme. Lower the heat and cook for 10 to 12 minutes, until the vegetables are well browned. Slowly pour in the red wine, scraping the browned bits from the bottom of the pan. Simmer until the liquid in the pan is reduced by half. Add the beef stock and check for salt and pepper. Add the short ribs back to the pan, along with any juices that have accumulated in the dish. Nestle all the ingredients together and place the lid on the pan. Move the pan to the oven and bake for 2 hours. Remove from the oven and allow the mixture to cool. When the short ribs are cool enough to handle, pull out the bones (they should slide right off the meat) and remove the bay leaves and thyme stems. Shred the meat with two forks, add in the bok choy, and mix well with the cooked vegetables. If the mixture seems dry, add more beef stock, a few tablespoons at a time, until the mixture is moist but not wet. Let cool completely.

While the short ribs are braising, make the pickled red onion. Add the onion to a large bowl. In a small saucepan, combine the water, red wine vinegar and sugar. Bring the mixture to a full boil, then drop the temperature and simmer for 5 minutes. Turn off the heat and carefully pour the pickling liquid over the red onion. Let the onion cool completely before using. Extra pickled red onion can be stored in the refrigerator for up to 2 weeks.

(continued)

DUMPLINGS

¼ cup (32 g) all-purpose flour

1 tsp kosher salt, plus more to taste

½ tsp black pepper, plus more to taste

½ tsp garlic powder

2 lbs (908 g) short ribs

4 tbsp (60 ml) olive oil, divided

1 stalk celery, diced

2 small carrots, diced

½ medium onion, diced

3 cloves garlic, minced

2 bay leaves

2–3 sprigs fresh thyme

½ cup (120 ml) dry red wine

1 cup (240 ml) low-sodium beef stock, plus more if needed

2 small bulbs bok choy, shredded

24 wonton skins, rolled thick

3 oz (85 g) provolone, thin sliced then cubed

QUICK PICKLED RED ONION

½ red onion, finely diced

½ cup (120 ml) water

½ cup (120 ml) red wine vinegar

2 tbsp (30 g) sugar

Short Rib Stacked Dumplings (cont.)

Preheat the oven to 400°F (200°C). Fill a small bowl with water and set aside. Line a baking sheet with parchment paper and spray with cooking spray; set aside.

To make the dumplings, lay a wonton dough square on a clean work surface at an angle, so that it looks like a diamond. Place a scant tablespoon (12 g) of the short-rib filling in the center of the square, top with ¼ teaspoon of pickled red onion, then top the onions with a heaping teaspoon of provolone cheese. Wet your fingers in the small bowl of water and wet down all four sides of the dumpling dough, then pull together the top and bottom points of the dough and squeeze together to seal. Pull the point on the right side up to the center and seal, then pull the left point to the center and seal. Your dumpling will resemble a pyramid. Place the finished dumpling on the parchment-lined sheet pan and cover with a tea towel or damp paper towel to keep them moist while working. Continue making dumplings until you have used all the filling and wrappers.

Bake the dumplings on the baking tray for 8 minutes, until they are just beginning to brown (they will continue to brown a bit when you pull them from the oven) and crisp up. Serve immediately.

Monte Cristo Dumplings

A Monte Cristo is a classic brunch sandwich that marries ham and cheese with sweetness. It is enjoyed as a break from the everyday French toast. It consists of a ham and Swiss cheese sandwich fried like French toast, then sprinkled with powdered sugar. It is often served with fruit preserves, which we reconceptualized as a red currant jam for dipping. Sprinkled sugar is traditional, and it. is. so. good. We recommend frying the dumplings for this one—steaming just doesn't crisp the dumplings up enough. You don't have to use the powdered sugar, or the jam—but it is really a treat. Sweet and savory is a great combo!

In a medium bowl, combine the shredded ham, turkey and Swiss cheese. Set aside.

In a small pot, melt the butter and cook for 2 to 3 minutes until it just begins to brown and smells nutty. Whisk in the Dijon mustard, then add the mixture to the bowl with the meats and cheese. Stir to coat well. Place in the refrigerator to cool and set up for 15 minutes.

Lay out a wonton square with the points pointing up and down. Place 1 tablespoon (15 g) of the chilled filling mixture in the center of the square. Dip your fingers in a small bowl of water and using a damp finger, wet down the outside edges of the wrapper and lift it into the palm of your hand. Fold the bottom point up to the top and seal the wonton, pressing out the excess air. You should now have a triangle. Place the folded dumplings on a sheet pan and cover with a towel to keep moist. Continue with the remaining filling and dough.

In a small bowl, combine the egg, milk, salt and nutmeg; set aside. Place a large heavy pan over medium–high heat and add the soybean oil. Heat the oil until it just begins to shimmer. Take one dumpling and dip it into the egg mixture, making sure to coat all sides. Shake off the excess egg wash and gently place the dumpling into the oil (the oil will only come partway up the dumpling; this technique is known as a shallow fry). Let the dumpling fry for 2 to 3 minutes, then gently flip the dumpling over and fry the second side. Once lightly browned on all sides, remove the dumpling from the oil and let it drain on paper towels. Continue with the remaining dumplings.

To serve, sprinkle with confectioners' sugar if using, and serve with red currant jam on the side for dipping.

YIELD: 24 DUMPLINGS

½ lb (227 g) deli ham, sliced thin and then shredded

½ lb (227 g) deli turkey, sliced thin and then shredded

¼ lb (113 g) Swiss cheese, sliced thin and then finely diced

4 tbsp (56 g) unsalted butter

2 tsp (10 ml) Dijon mustard

24 wonton wrappers, rolled thick

1 large egg, lightly beaten

1 tbsp (15 ml) whole milk

Pinch of kosher salt

Pinch of ground nutmeg

1 cup (240 ml) soybean oil

Confectioners' sugar, for garnish (optional)

Red currant jam, for dipping (optional)

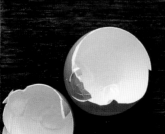

Pan-Fried Beef Dumplings

YIELD: 24 DUMPLINGS

1 tbsp (15 ml) olive oil

2 carrots, finely diced

4 oz (114 g) white button mushrooms, stems removed and finely diced

1 (2-inch [5-cm]) piece of fresh ginger, peeled and minced

3 green onions, trimmed, white and green parts sliced thinly

1 tsp kosher salt

½ tsp black pepper

1½ lbs (680 g) 80/20 ground beef

3 large eggs, lightly beaten

3 tbsp (45 ml) soy sauce, plus extra for dipping finished dumplings

1 tsp oyster sauce

2 tsp (10 ml) toasted sesame oil

24 wonton wrappers, rolled thick

1 cup (240 ml) soybean oil

Ok . . . getting down to basics. This is a really good dumpling for beef lovers. It has some mushrooms, some carrots, a little oyster sauce for depth. Super good. These fry up crispy and are served with a basic soy sauce dipper. You can add some chives for color, but honestly, these are good plain. I like pairing these dumplings with red wine.

Place a large sauté pan over medium–high heat and add the olive oil. Add the carrots and mushrooms and cook, stirring occasionally, for 10 minutes, until the carrots begin to soften and the mushrooms begin to give up their liquids. Add the ginger, green onions, salt and pepper, and cook for an additional 5 minutes. Then add the vegetables to a large bowl with the ground beef.

Place the pan back over the heat and pour the beaten eggs into the pan (don't wipe out the pan—the leftover oil from cooking the vegetables will be enough to keep the eggs from sticking!). Tilt the pan around so that the eggs cover the entire bottom of the pan in a thin layer and cook for 2 to 3 minutes until cooked through and dry on top. Slide the egg pancake out of the pan and cut it into tiny pieces. Add the egg to the bowl with the beef and cooked vegetables.

To the bowl, add the soy sauce, oyster sauce and toasted sesame oil. Using clean hands, mix well so that the fillings are evenly distributed through the meat.

Lay a wonton dough square on a clean work surface at an angle, so that it looks like a diamond. Place 1 heaping teaspoon of the beef filling in the center of the wonton square. Wet your fingers in a small bowl of water and run a damp finger along all four outside edges of the wrapper.

Carefully pick up the wonton skin and lay it in the palm of your hand, keeping the points pointing up toward your middle finger and down to the base of your palm. Gently fold the bottom point of the skin up over the filling, creating a triangle, then gently press the seams to close them well. Using the tip of your finger, wet the two diagonal sides and begin sealing the seam on the left side making small folds from the left side slightly over the right (similar to crimping a pie crust). Remember to line up the edges of the wrapper as you pleat and press all the way around. Continue pleating seven to ten times until the dumpling is completely sealed. The finished dumpling will have a half-moon shape. (See more on page 58.) Place the finished dumpling on a sheet pan and cover with a tea towel or damp paper towel to keep them moist while working. Continue making dumplings until you have used all the filling and wrappers.

Place a large deep pot over high heat and add the soybean oil. Heat the oil to 360°F (180°C). Carefully fry the dumplings in batches of six in the oil for about 8 minutes until well browned—be sure to fry for at least 8 minutes so the meat filling cooks completely during this step. Don't fry more than six dumplings at a time or you will lower the temperature of the oil too fast and your dumplings will be oily and greasy, not crispy! Drain the dumplings on paper towels and serve with extra soy sauce for dipping.

French Dip Dumplings

My absolute favorite diner sandwich is a French Dip. I like the crusty bread dripping with au jus, and I love the melty cheese oozing from the sides. I thought it would make a good dumpling and I was right! The au jus is a good dumpling sauce. Be careful to use unsalted butter, and grill seasoning is essential to keep it flavorful. I try to use drinking sherry instead of cooking sherry—it's less salty.

YIELD: 24 DUMPLINGS

1½ lbs (680 g) deli-style roast beef, sliced thin

2 tsp (10 g) grill seasoning of your choice

2 tbsp (28 g) unsalted butter

1 shallot, finely minced

¼ cup (60 ml) dry sherry

1 tbsp (8 g) all-purpose flour

1½ cups (360 ml) beef consommé, or low-sodium beef broth

24 wonton wrappers, rolled thin

2–3 tbsp (30–45 ml) soybean oil, divided

Fill a small bowl with water and set aside.

On a cutting board, chop the roast beef well and then toss it with the grill seasoning. Place the meat mixture in the refrigerator and let it chill for at least 30 minutes and up to 2 hours.

Place a medium saucepan over high heat, and add the butter and shallot. Cook for 8 to 10 minutes, until the shallot is softened and just beginning to brown. Take the pan off the heat, slowly pour in the sherry, and place the pan back over the heat. Cook for 5 to 6 minutes, until almost all the sherry is gone and the pan is almost dry. Sprinkle the flour over the shallot and cook, stirring constantly, for 4 to 5 minutes to cook out the raw flour. Slowly pour in the beef consommé (or beef broth), whisking constantly to prevent lumps from forming. Simmer over low heat for 10 to 15 minutes until the sauce is slightly thickened and glossy. Set aside half of this au jus for dipping the finished wontons and toss the beef in the other half of the au jus to coat. The beef should be wet, but not soggy.

Lay a wonton dough square on a clean work surface at an angle, so that it looks like a diamond. Place 1 heaping teaspoon of filling in the center of the wonton square. Wet your fingers in the small bowl of water and run a damp finger along all four outside edges of the wrapper.

Carefully pick up the wonton skin and lay it in the palm of your hand, keeping the points pointing up toward your middle finger and down to the base of your palm. Gently fold the bottom point of the skin up over the filling, creating a triangle, then gently press the seams to close them well. Using the tip of your finger, wet the two diagonal sides and begin sealing the seam on the left side making small folds from the left side slightly over the right (similar to crimping a pie crust). Remember to line up the edges of the wrapper as you pleat and press all the way around. Continue pleating seven to ten times until the dumpling is completely sealed. The finished dumpling will have a half-moon shape. (See more on page 58.) Place the finished dumpling on a sheet pan and cover with a tea towel or damp paper towel to keep them moist while working. Continue making dumplings until you have used all the filling and wrappers.

Place a large sauté pan over medium–high heat. Add 1 to 2 tablespoons (15 to 30 ml) of soybean oil to the pan and heat until the oil shimmers. Place six to eight dumplings in the pan and fry for 3 to 4 minutes until crispy and browned. Carefully pour in ¼ cup (60 ml) of water and cover the pan with a lid. Let the dumplings steam for 3 to 4 minutes. Cook the rest of the dumplings in batches of six to eight, adding more oil as necessary. Serve with the reserved au jus for dipping.

The Amazing Impossible™ Burger Wontons

1 lb (454 g) Impossible™ burger meat

½ onion, minced

3 cloves garlic, minced

4 oz (113 g) white cheddar, shredded

2 tbsp (30 ml) ketchup, plus more for garnish

2 tbsp (30 ml) yellow mustard, plus more for garnish

½ tsp kosher salt

¼ tsp black pepper

24 wonton wrappers, rolled thick

What is an Impossible™ burger? Well . . . it's a burger made from a plant-based meat substitute, and looks and tastes just like hamburger. It is vegan and can be used in any recipe instead of beef. People concerned with the environmental impact of beef can still have a burger wonton! Mix it with condiments and cheese, and you have a vegetarian option that is fun and delicious. Omit the cheese if you want to keep it completely vegan.

Fill a small bowl with water and set aside.

In a large bowl, combine the Impossible burger meat, onion, garlic, shredded cheddar, ketchup, mustard, salt and pepper. Mix well to combine.

Lay out a wonton square with the points pointing up and down. Place 1 tablespoon (15 g) of the filling mixture in the center of the square. Dip your fingers in the small bowl of water and using a damp finger, wet down the outside edges of the wrapper and lift it into the palm of your hand. Fold the bottom point up to the top and seal the wonton, pressing out the excess air. You should now have a triangle. Wet the bottom points and fold them in on each other to create a tortellini-shaped wonton (see more on page 54). Place the finished dumplings on a parchment-lined sheet pan and cover with a towel. Repeat with the remaining wonton squares and filling.

Set a steamer basket over a pot of simmering water. Place eight to ten dumplings into the basket and close the lid. Steam the dumplings for 10 to 12 minutes, until the filling is cooked through and the skins are tightly formed around the filling.

Serve the dumplings garnished with ketchup and mustard.

Pork, Lamb & Turkey Dumplings

Go Greek Gyro Dumplings

YIELD: 24 DUMPLINGS

A gyro is a beautiful thing. It is a meat, usually lamb, cooked on a vertical spit, which imparts a lot of flavor. The sandwich is served on a pita, with tomatoes, onions and a delectable sauce called tzatziki, which is made out of yogurt and mint. Gyros turn into a nice dumpling easily, and the sauce in these is super refreshing. A little yogurt, a little mint and grated cucumber (which makes the sauce a lot smoother) help us reimagine the classic. It's a fabulous take. Your local butcher can grind the lamb for you and if you aren't a lamb fan, you can use ground beef instead.

TZATZIKI

½ cup (96 g) Greek yogurt (plain)

½ seedless cucumber, grated on a box grater and squeezed through paper towels to drain out excess water

Juice and zest of 1 lemon

1 tbsp (1 g) fresh dill

1 tbsp (1 g) fresh mint

⅛ tsp cayenne (optional)

¼ tsp kosher salt

¼ tsp black pepper

DUMPLINGS

1 lb (454 g) ground lamb

1 tbsp (15 ml) olive oil

¼ cup (40 g) onion, minced

2–3 cloves garlic, minced

1 tsp dried mint

1 tsp dried oregano

1 tsp kosher salt

½ tsp black pepper

24 wonton wrappers, rolled thin

3–4 tbsp (45–60 ml) soybean oil, divided

To make the tzatziki, in a small bowl, combine the Greek yogurt, cucumber, lemon juice and zest, dill, mint and cayenne (if using). Season with the salt and pepper. Refrigerate for at least 30 minutes to allow the flavors to come together.

To make the dumpling filling, in a large bowl, combine the ground lamb with the olive oil, onion, garlic, mint, oregano, salt and pepper and mix until well combined.

Fill a small bowl with water and set aside.

Lay a wonton dough square on a clean work surface at an angle, so that it looks like a diamond. Place 1 heaping teaspoon of the lamb filling in the center of the wonton square. Wet your fingers in the small bowl of water and run a damp finger along all four outside edges of the wrapper.

Carefully pick up the wonton skin and lay it in the palm of your hand, keeping the points pointing up toward your middle finger and down to the base of your palm. Gently fold the bottom point of the skin up over the filling, creating a triangle, then gently press the seams to close them well. Using the tip of your finger, wet the two diagonal sides and begin sealing the seam on the left side making small folds from the left side slightly over the right (similar to crimping a pie crust). Remember to line up the edges of the wrapper as you pleat and press all the way around. Continue pleating seven to ten times until the dumpling is completely sealed. The finished dumpling will have a half-moon shape. (See more on page 58.) Place the finished dumpling on a sheet pan and cover with a tea towel or damp paper towel to keep them moist while working. Continue making dumplings until you have used all the filling and wrappers.

Place a large sauté pan with a tight-fitting lid over medium–high heat. Add 1 to 2 tablespoons (15 to 30 ml) of the soybean oil to the pan and heat to a shimmer. Add six to eight dumplings to the pan and cook for 4 to 5 minutes, until the bottoms of the dumplings are brown and crispy. Carefully pour ¼ cup (60 ml) of water into the pan and cover the pan with a lid. Let the dumplings steam for 3 to 4 minutes, until the filling is cooked through and the skin has formed a tight seal (the dumplings should lift easily from the bottom of the pan). Cook the rest of the dumplings in batches of six to eight, adding more oil as necessary.

Serve immediately with the tzatziki.

Mom's Three-Meat Dumplings

Every Tuesday night growing up was Mom's meatloaf for dinner. Meatloaf takes you back to a simpler time, and this version of it as a dumpling is both hearty and clearly all American. This dumpling is super nostalgic and fun to make. It's not fancy, but that's the point. We took this classic dish and put our own spin on it. We call it the Three-Meat Dumpling because it's a traditional one-third meatloaf mix used in the filling. Yum.

The sauce is really good, but ketchup can also be used as a dipping sauce. It's sometimes fun to play around and suit your own taste.

In a medium bowl, combine the meatloaf mix (or combined ground meats) with the onion, garlic, ketchup, Dijon mustard, oregano, salt and pepper and mix well to combine.

To make the dipping sauce, combine the Worcestershire sauce, sesame oil, soy sauce and Sriracha in a small bowl. Set aside.

Fill a small bowl with water and set aside.

Lay a wonton dough square on a clean work surface at an angle, so that it looks like a diamond. Place 1 heaping teaspoon of the meatloaf filling in the center of the wonton square. Wet your fingers in the small bowl of water and run a damp finger along all four outside edges of the wrapper.

Carefully pick up the wonton skin and lay it in the palm of your hand, keeping the points pointing up toward your middle finger and down to the base of your palm. Gently fold the bottom point of the skin up over the filling, creating a triangle, then gently press the seams to close them well. Using the tip of your finger, wet the two diagonal sides and begin sealing the seam on the left side making small folds from the left side slightly over the right (similar to crimping a pie crust). Remember to line up the edges of the wrapper as you pleat and press all the way around. Continue pleating seven to ten times until the dumpling is completely sealed. The finished dumpling will have a half-moon shape. (See more on page 58.) Place the finished dumpling on a sheet pan and cover with a tea towel or damp paper towel to keep them moist while working. Continue making dumplings until you have used all the filling and wrappers.

Place a large sauté pan with a tight-fitting lid over medium–high heat. Add 1 to 2 tablespoons (15 to 30 ml) of the soybean oil to the pan and heat to a shimmer, 3 to 4 minutes. Add six to eight dumplings to the pan at a time to prevent crowding and cook for 4 to 5 minutes, until the bottoms of the dumplings are brown and crispy. Carefully pour ¼ cup (60 ml) of water into the pan and cover the pan with a lid. Let the dumplings steam for 3 to 4 minutes, until the filling is cooked through and the skin has formed a tight seal (the dumplings should lift easily from the bottom of the pan). Cook the rest of the dumplings in batches of six to eight, adding more oil as necessary.

Serve immediately with ketchup or dipping sauce.

FILLING

1 lb (454 g) meatloaf mix (or ⅓ lb [150 g] ground beef, ⅓ lb [150 g] ground pork and ⅓ lb [150 g] ground veal)

½ onion, diced

1–2 cloves garlic, minced

2 tbsp (30 ml) ketchup

1 tsp Dijon mustard

1 tsp dried oregano

½ tsp kosher salt

¼ tsp black pepper

24 wonton wrappers, rolled thin

3–4 tbsp (45–60 ml) soybean oil, divided

DIPPING SAUCE

4 tbsp (60 ml) Worcestershire sauce

4 tbsp (60 ml) sesame oil

3 tbsp (45 ml) soy sauce

1 tsp Sriracha

Ketchup, to serve (optional)

Roasted Squash & Pork Dumplings

YIELD: 24 DUMPLINGS

½ small butternut squash, peeled and diced into ¼-inch (6-mm) cubes

1 red apple of your choice, peeled and diced into ¼-inch (6-mm) cubes

2 tbsp (30 ml) vegetable oil

½ tsp kosher salt

¼ tsp black pepper

1 lb (454 g) ground pork

3 tbsp (45 ml) maple syrup

3 scallions, thinly sliced

1 egg white

24 wonton wrappers, rolled thick

These roasted squash and pork dumplings are really, really good, and our homage to fall. They are based on recipes from New York State's Hudson Valley, which is known for its rustic local food and leaf peeping. These dumplings are savory–sweet and would be great for Thanksgiving or Christmas Eve. The maple syrup in these dumplings is unexpected, but it pairs perfectly with both the squash and pork, and the apples add a little crunch and texture. The squash adds some additional sweetness and reminds me of a fall casserole.

Preheat the oven to 375°F (190°C). Line a sheet pan with parchment paper and set aside.

In a small bowl, combine the cubed butternut squash and cubed apple with the vegetable oil, salt and pepper and toss to coat well. Spread the squash and apple in a single layer on the sheet pan and roast for 20 to 25 minutes, until the squash and apple are soft and just beginning to brown. Let cool slightly. Leave the oven set to 375°F (190°C).

In a large bowl, combine the roasted squash and apple with the ground pork, maple syrup, scallions and egg white, using your hands to mix well to combine thoroughly.

Fill a small bowl with water and set aside.

Lay a wonton dough square on a clean work surface at an angle, so that it looks like a diamond. Place 1 heaping teaspoon of the squash and pork filling in the center of the wonton square. Wet your fingers in the small bowl of water and run a damp finger along all four outside edges of the wrapper.

Carefully pick up the wonton skin and lay it in the palm of your hand, keeping the points pointing up toward your middle finger and down to the base of your palm. Gently fold the bottom point of the skin up over the filling, creating a triangle, then gently press the seams to close them well. Using the tip of your finger, wet the two diagonal sides and begin sealing the seam on the left side making small folds from the left side slightly over the right (similar to crimping a pie crust). Remember to line up the edges of the wrapper as you pleat and press all the way around. Continue pleating seven to ten times until the dumpling is completely sealed. The finished dumpling will have a half-moon shape. (See more on page 58.) Place the finished dumpling on a sheet pan and cover with a tea towel or damp paper towel to keep them moist while working. Continue making dumplings until you have used all the filling and wrappers.

When you have finished forming the dumplings, place the sheet pan back into the oven and bake for 8 to 10 minutes, until the dumplings are lightly browned and crispy. Serve immediately.

Bacon, Egg & Cheese Dumplings

Every corner in New York City has a breakfast truck, which serves the quintessential bacon, egg and cheese. Every sandwich is on a kaiser roll, and you get the same sandwich all over the city. Some like it with ketchup, some like it without, but it has to be on a roll, and with cheese. Those are the rules. Our version of it has taken liberties by adding candied bacon—this is an homage to the fact that most griddles are used for everything, and the syrup ends up flavoring the bacon. It's delicious. The sweet and savory flavors mingling are pretty addictive. Take your time with the eggs so that they cook evenly. The number of eggs in this recipe will take a little time to cook, but it's worth it.

YIELD: 24 DUMPLINGS

8 slices thick-cut bacon

2 tbsp (30 ml) maple syrup

6 tbsp (84 g) unsalted butter

8 large eggs, lightly beaten

8 oz (227 g) sharp cheddar cheese, shredded

24 circular wonton wrappers, rolled thick

1 cup (240 ml) soybean oil

Place a large pan over medium–high heat, and cook the bacon until it renders most of its fat and is well browned on both sides, 10 to 12 minutes. Alternatively, you can lay the bacon on a cooling rack placed on a baking sheet and bake the bacon at 400°F (200°C) for 12 to 15 minutes. Remove the bacon from pan and drain it on paper towels. Drizzle the bacon with maple syrup and let it cool for 10 minutes. Chop the candied bacon into a fine dice and set aside.

Place a large nonstick sauté pan over medium heat. Add the butter to the pan and let it melt and begin to bubble slightly. Add the beaten eggs and cook, stirring constantly, until soft curds begin to form, 8 to 10 minutes. Add the candied bacon and shredded cheddar to the eggs and continue cooking, stirring occasionally, for another 4 to 5 minutes. The eggs should be fully cooked and dry, not runny.

Fill a small bowl with water and set aside.

Place 1 heaping teaspoon of the filling in the center of the wonton. Fold the dough up the sides of the mixture but don't cover the top. Dip your finger in the small bowl of water. Run your finger along the outer rim of the dough. Carefully fold the dough over itself, similar to crimping a pie crust, to create the classic shumai style (see more on page 25). Place the finished dumpling on a sheet pan and cover with a tea towel or damp paper towel to keep them moist while working. Continue making dumplings until you have used all the filling and wrappers.

Place a deep, heavy pan over high heat. Add the soybean oil and heat it to 365°F (185°C). Carefully place four to six dumplings into the hot oil (frying too many dumplings at one time will lower the oil temperature and make your dumplings greasy instead of crispy). Fry the dumplings on one side for 3 to 4 minutes, until light brown, then flip and fry on the second side for another 3 to 4 minutes. Drain the dumplings on paper towels and continue with the remaining dumplings. Serve immediately.

Pork & Wild Mushroom Dumplings

YIELD: 24 DUMPLINGS

DUMPLINGS

2 tbsp (30 ml) sesame oil (dark or light)

4 oz (113 g) fresh shiitake mushrooms, stems discarded and caps thinly sliced

1 tbsp (6 g) fresh ginger, peeled and grated

1 tbsp (15 g) garlic, minced

¾ cup (70 g) scallions, sliced thin

3 tbsp (45 ml) soy sauce

2 tbsp (30 ml) hoisin sauce

½ tsp black pepper

1 lb (454 g) ground pork

24 wonton wrappers, rolled thin

3–4 tbsp (45–60 ml) soybean oil, divided

DIPPING SAUCE

¼ cup (60 ml) hot water

2 tbsp (28 g) light brown sugar

2 tbsp (30 ml) rice wine vinegar

2 tbsp (30 ml) soy sauce

1 tbsp (15 ml) sambal oelek (or as much or as little as you prefer)

1 scallion, sliced thin

Shiitake mushrooms are fragrant and meaty and used in a variety of dishes. This dumpling pairs exceptionally well with the Roasted Squash & Pork Dumplings (page 46). These can make a feast that is really comforting. You can substitute Sriracha, which is easier to find, for the sambal oelek.

Place a large sauté pan over medium–high heat and add the sesame oil. When the oil is heated add the mushrooms in a single layer. Let the mushrooms cook for 6 to 8 minutes without moving them, until the mushrooms begin to brown. Add the ginger, garlic and scallions and let the mixture cook for another 5 to 6 minutes, until the scallions are wilted and fragrant. Transfer the vegetables to a medium bowl and add the soy sauce, hoisin sauce, pepper and ground pork. Mix well with your hands until the mixture is well combined.

Lay a wonton dough square on a clean work surface at an angle, so that it looks like a diamond. Place 1 heaping teaspoon of the pork and mushroom filling in the center of the wonton square. Wet your fingers in a small bowl of water and run a damp finger along all four outside edges of the wrapper.

Carefully pick up the wonton skin and lay it in the palm of your hand, keeping the points pointing up toward your middle finger and down to the base of your palm. Gently fold the bottom point of the skin up over the filling, creating a triangle, then gently press the seams to close them well. Using the tip of your finger, wet the two diagonal sides and begin sealing the seam on the left side making small folds from the left side slightly over the right (similar to crimping a pie crust). Remember to line up the edges of the wrapper as you pleat and press all the way around. Continue pleating seven to ten times until the dumpling is completely sealed. The finished dumpling will have a half-moon shape. (See more on page 58.) Place the finished dumpling on a sheet pan and cover with a tea towel or damp paper towel to keep them moist while working. Continue making dumplings until you have used all the filling and wrappers.

Place a large sauté pan with a tight-fitting lid over medium–high heat. Add 1 to 2 tablespoons (15 to 30 ml) of the soybean oil to the pan and heat to a shimmer, 3 to 4 minutes. Add six to eight dumplings to the pan at a time to prevent crowding and cook for 4 to 5 minutes, until the bottoms of the dumplings are brown and crispy. Carefully pour ¼ cup (60 ml) of water into the pan and cover the pan with a lid. Let the dumplings steam for 3 to 4 minutes, until the filling is cooked through and the skin has formed a tight seal (the dumplings should lift easily from the bottom of the pan). Cook the rest of the dumplings in batches of six to eight, adding more oil as necessary.

To make the sauce, combine the hot water and brown sugar in a small bowl and stir to dissolve. Whisk in the rice wine vinegar and soy sauce and as much or little sambal oelek as you would like. Top with sliced scallion and serve with dumplings.

Chinese Lamb Dumplings

Lamb is traditionally a spring dish, but these hearty lamb dumplings have a touch of cumin and coriander for depth and are well suited for fall and winter menus. These are a sophisticated take on dumplings and make for a delicious dinner.

Place a large sauté pan over medium–high heat, add the vegetable oil to the pan and heat until the oil starts to shimmer. Add the red onion and cook for 2 to 3 minutes, then add the cabbage and continue cooking for another 8 to 10 minutes, until the cabbage is wilted and the volume has reduced by half. Remove the onion and cabbage from the pan and drain in a colander for a few minutes until all of the excess water has drained out. Place the cabbage and onion in a medium bowl. Add the chives, Worcestershire sauce, cumin, ground coriander, salt and pepper. Toss well, then add the ground lamb. Using your hands, mix the vegetables and spices into the lamb.

To make the sauce, combine the soy sauce, scallion and ginger in a small bowl and set aside to let the flavors meld.

Fill a small bowl with water and set aside.

Lay a wonton dough square on a clean work surface at an angle, so that it looks like a diamond. Place 1 heaping teaspoon of the lamb filling in the center of the wonton square. Wet your fingers in the small bowl of water and run a damp finger along all four outside edges of the wrapper.

Carefully pick up the wonton skin and lay it in the palm of your hand, keeping the points pointing up toward your middle finger and down to the base of your palm. Gently fold the bottom point of the skin up over the filling, creating a triangle, then gently press the seams to close them well. Using the tip of your finger, wet the two diagonal sides and begin sealing the seam on the left side making small folds from the left side slightly over the right (similar to crimping a pie crust). Remember to line up the edges of the wrapper as you pleat and press all the way around. Continue pleating seven to ten times until the dumpling is completely sealed. The finished dumpling will have a half-moon shape. (See more on page 58.) Place the finished dumpling on a sheet pan and cover with a tea towel or damp paper towel to keep them moist while working. Continue making dumplings until you have used all the filling and wrappers.

Place a large sauté pan with a tight-fitting lid over medium–high heat. Add 1 to 2 tablespoons (15 to 30 ml) of the soybean oil to the pan and heat to a shimmer, 3 to 4 minutes. Add six to eight dumplings to the pan at a time to prevent crowding and cook for 4 to 5 minutes, until the bottoms of the dumplings are brown and crispy. Carefully pour ¼ cup (60 ml) of water into the pan and cover the pan with a lid. Let the dumplings steam for 3 to 4 minutes, until the filling is cooked through and the skin has formed a tight seal (the dumplings should lift easily from the bottom of the pan). Cook the rest of the dumplings in batches of six to eight, adding more oil as necessary.

Serve immediately with the dipping sauce.

YIELD: 24 DUMPLINGS

DUMPLINGS

2 tbsp (30 ml) vegetable oil

½ red onion, diced

½ cup (35 g) Napa cabbage, finely shredded

½ bunch chives, finely chopped

2 tbsp (30 ml) Worcestershire sauce

1 tsp cumin

½ tsp ground coriander

¾ tsp kosher salt

¼ tsp black pepper

1 lb (454 g) ground lamb

24 wonton wrappers, rolled thin

3–4 tbsp (45–60 ml) soybean oil, divided

DIPPING SAUCE

4 tbsp (60 ml) soy sauce

1 scallion, sliced thin

1 tsp fresh ginger, peeled and minced

Fried Pork & Bok Choy Dumplings

YIELD: 24 DUMPLINGS

DUMPLINGS

1 large head bok choy, trimmed and shredded

1 tsp kosher salt

2–3 scallions, roughly chopped

1½ lbs (680 g) ground pork

1 tbsp (15 ml) soy sauce

1 tbsp (15 ml) shaoxing wine (or seasoned rice wine vinegar)

2 tsp (10 g) sugar

24 wonton wrappers, rolled thick

1 cup (240 ml) soybean oil

DIPPING SAUCE

2 tbsp (30 ml) soy sauce

2 tbsp (30 ml) seasoned rice wine vinegar

2 scallions, thinly sliced

1 tbsp (6 g) fresh ginger, grated

Fried pork dumplings are a Chinese takeout classic. I have yet to meet anyone who doesn't love traditional pork dumplings. My favorite place to get them in Chinatown is a tiny hole in the wall, where you can get eight dumplings for a dollar. It's one of the best-kept culinary secrets in New York City and there's a little park nearby where you can sit and enjoy them. I like bok choy because it's milder than cabbage but still retains its crunch. You can substitute cabbage, though, if you prefer.

Place the shredded bok choy in a colander and toss with the salt, to take out excess water. Let the bok choy drain for at least 20 minutes, then transfer to the bowl of a food processor. Add the scallions, ground pork, soy sauce, shaoxing wine (or seasoned rice wine vinegar) and sugar. Using the pulse option, process the mixture until it becomes a paste. Transfer the mixture to a bowl and chill in the refrigerator for at least 20 minutes.

To make the dipping sauce, combine the soy sauce, rice wine vinegar, scallions and ginger in a small bowl and let the mixture sit to allow the flavors to meld.

Fill a small bowl with water and set aside. Line a sheet pan with parchment paper and set aside.

Lay out a wonton square with the points pointing up and down. Place 1 tablespoon (15 g) of the chilled filling mixture in the center of the square. Dip your fingers in the small bowl of water and using a damp finger, wet down the outside edges of the wrapper and lift it into the palm of your hand. Fold the bottom point up to the top and seal the wonton, pressing out the excess air. You should now have a triangle. Wet the bottom points and fold them in on each other to create a tortellini-shaped wonton. Place the finished dumplings on the parchment-lined sheet pan and cover with a towel. Repeat with the remaining wonton squares and filling.

Place a deep, heavy pan over medium–high heat, add the soybean oil and heat the oil until it shimmers. Carefully place six to eight wontons into the hot oil (frying too many wontons at once will lower the temperature of the oil too fast, and your wontons will be greasy instead of crispy). Let the dumplings fry 4 to 5 minutes on each side, until lightly browned and crispy. Drain on paper towels and continue with the rest of the dumplings.

Serve immediately with the dipping sauce.

Five-Spice Pork Dumplings

Every home kitchen should have spice blends on hand to experiment with different flavors. Five-spice powder blends are available in every grocery store, and they are an easy way to add exoticism. There are some dumplings in this book that are perfect as hors d'oeuvres for more elegant meals, and these dumplings fit that bill. They are a great starter to a classic steak dinner, and the hoisin sauce is always a hit. Hoisin, by the way, is a plum sauce that is a little smoky and similar to an Asian BBQ sauce. It's sweet, and the contrast between the hoisin and five-spice powder is a classic. You can find all of these ingredients in the Asian section of most grocery stores.

In a medium bowl, combine the hoisin sauce, soy sauce, sambal oelek, five-spice powder and sesame oil. Remove 1 to 2 tablespoons (15 to 30 ml) of the sauce to a small bowl and set aside for serving. To the remaining sauce add the pork, crumbled tofu, chives and black pepper, then mix well to combine.

Fill a small bowl with water and set aside.

Place a wonton wrapper on a clean surface. Place 1 tablespoon (15 g) of the filling in the center of each wrapper. Dip your fingers in the small bowl of water and using a damp finger, wet the outer edges. Bring the left-hand top and bottom points together and squeeze to seal. Bring the right-hand point up to meet the first points and squeeze all the seams tightly to make sure the dumpling is sealed into a 3D triangle shape. Place the finished dumplings on a sheet pan and cover with a towel. Repeat with the remaining wonton wrappers and filling.

Set a steamer basket over a pot of simmering water. Place eight to ten dumplings into the basket and close the lid. Steam for 10 to 12 minutes, until the filling is cooked through and the skins are tightly formed around the filling. Remove the dumplings from the basket, and top with a drop of the reserved hoisin–chili sauce to serve.

YIELD: 24 DUMPLINGS

¼ cup (60 ml) hoisin sauce

2 tbsp (30 ml) soy sauce

1½ tsp (8 ml) sambal oelek, or chili garlic sauce of choice

½ tsp five-spice powder

¼ tsp sesame oil

¾ lb (340 g) ground pork

6 oz (170 g) soft tofu, crumbled

4 tbsp (12 g) chopped chives

¼ tsp black pepper

24 circular wonton wrappers, rolled thin

Turkey Club Dumplings

The club sandwich was first written about in 1889. There are two places it may have originated—New York City or Saratoga, New York—and it was served in quarters, rising high, with a toothpick holding it together, so you could pick it up. It had three slices of white toast, turkey, tomato and bacon and it was on every menu in every diner. Actually, it still is. We have amped up the flavor a little with these dumplings, and yet it still retains its roots, with the smokiness of the bacon set off by the mild turkey. We also added a little zing with the plum sauce. Sounds weird, tastes amazing!

YIELD: 24 DUMPLINGS

1 lb (454 g) ground turkey

2 medium slicing tomatoes, roughly chopped

2 slices Monterey Jack or Swiss cheese, sliced into sticks then chopped

4 slices bacon, cooked until crispy and crumbled

3–4 bulbs bok choy, trimmed, core removed and shredded

2 tbsp (30 ml) plum sauce

24 wonton wrappers, rolled thin

3–4 tbsp (45–60 ml) soybean oil

Combine the ground turkey, chopped tomatoes, cheese, crumbled bacon, bok choy and plum sauce in a large bowl and mix well to combine.

Fill a small bowl with water and set aside.

Lay the wonton dough on a clean work surface and place 1 heaping teaspoon of the turkey club filling in the center. Wet your fingers in the small bowl of water and run a damp finger along the outside edges of the wrapper.

Carefully pick up the wonton skin and lay it in the palm of your hand, keeping the points pointing up toward your middle finger and down to the base of your palm. Gently fold the bottom point of the skin up over the filling, creating a triangle, then gently press the seams to close them well. Using the tip of your finger, wet the two diagonal sides and begin sealing the seam on the left side making small folds from the left side slightly over the right (similar to crimping a pie crust). Remember to line up the edges of the wrapper as you pleat and press all the way around. Continue pleating seven to ten times until the dumpling is completely sealed. The finished dumpling will have a half-moon shape. Place the finished dumpling on a sheet pan and cover with a tea towel or damp paper towel to keep them moist while working. Continue making dumplings until you have used all the filling and wrappers.

Place a large sauté pan with a tight-fitting lid over medium–high heat. Add 1 to 2 tablespoons (15 to 30 ml) of the soybean oil to the pan and heat to a shimmer, 3 to 4 minutes. Add six to eight dumplings to the pan at a time to prevent crowding and cook for 4 to 5 minutes, until the bottoms of the dumplings are brown and crispy. Carefully pour ¼ cup (60 ml) of water into the pan and cover the pan with a lid. Let the dumplings steam for 3 to 4 minutes, until the filling is cooked through and the skin has formed a tight seal (the dumplings should lift easily from the bottom of the pan). Cook the rest of the dumplings in batches of six to eight, adding more oil as necessary.

Serve immediately.

Pork Spring Roll Dumplings

A Thai spring roll is filled with noodles—we call them "noods" around our house. Fish sauce isn't necessarily a staple in every house, but it adds a good depth of flavor to a lot of dishes. I first had fish sauce in Pad Thai, which is still my Friday night jam. This dish may sound exotic, but it is so easy and perfect for everyone who loves Thai food.

YIELD: 24 DUMPLINGS

1 oz (28 g) dried shiitake mushrooms

1 oz (28 g) dried cellophane rice noodles (also known as mung bean noodles)

8 oz (227 g) ground pork (or cooked, finely shredded pork tenderloin)

¼ cup (30 g) grated carrot

4 tbsp (10 g) fresh basil, chiffonade

4 tbsp (10 g) fresh mint, chiffonade

1 tsp fish sauce

¼ tsp kosher salt

¼ tsp black pepper

24 wonton wrappers, rolled thin

1 cup (240 ml) soybean oil

Bring 1 cup (240 ml) of water to a boil in a small saucepan, then add the dried shiitake mushrooms and simmer for 4 to 5 minutes. When the mushrooms have softened, carefully remove the mushrooms from the water, making sure to leave any dirt and silt in the pan. Remove and discard the stems of the mushrooms, chop the caps well and set aside.

Place the cellophane rice noodles in a medium bowl and pour boiling water over them. Let the noodles sit in the water for 10 minutes, until they are soft and pliable. Drain the noodles and, using scissors, snip the noodles into 1- to 2-inch (3- to 5-cm) pieces and set aside.

In a medium bowl, combine the ground pork (or shredded pork tenderloin if using), chopped mushrooms, sliced cellophane noodles, carrot, basil, mint, fish sauce, salt and pepper. Using your hands, mix well to combine. Let the mixture sit for 10 to 15 minutes for the flavors to meld.

Fill a small bowl with water and set aside. Line a sheet pan with parchment paper and set aside.

Lay a wonton square in a diamond shape, with the points pointing up and down. Place a tablespoon (15 g) of the pork filling in the center of the wrapper. Wet your fingers in the small bowl of water and run a damp finger along all four outside edges of the wrapper. Place the dumpling in the middle of your palm with the points facing up and down. Fold the bottom point up over the filling and line it up with the top point. Press all edges to seal well. Holding the dumpling in the palm of your hand, gently crimp the edges so that the dumpling forms a half-moon shape, making sure you seal them tight (see more on page 58). Place the finished dumplings on the parchment-lined sheet pan and cover with a towel. Repeat with the remaining wonton squares and filling.

Place a deep, heavy pan over medium–high heat, add the oil and heat until the oil begins to shimmer. Carefully place six to eight wontons into the hot oil (frying too many wontons at once will lower the temperature of the oil too fast, and your wontons will be greasy instead of crispy). Let the dumplings fry for 4 to 5 minutes, until lightly browned and crispy. Drain on paper towels and serve immediately.

Hot Italian Salami Dumplings

YIELD: 24 DUMPLINGS

8 slices dry salami, chopped

4 oz (114 g) provolone, chopped

2 oz (57 g) grated Parmesan

4 oz (114 g) bok choy, thinly sliced

2 scallions, thinly sliced

2 tbsp (30 ml) spicy brown mustard, plus more for serving

2 tbsp (28 g) mayonnaise

2–3 grinds of black pepper

24 wonton wrappers, rolled thick

3–4 tbsp (45–60 ml) soybean oil

As a major immigrant hub, New York City is the home of many cuisines. Foods tend to bleed into each other, and Italian is often the comfort food of everyone growing up in the area. A hot salami sandwich was what your grandma made when you wanted a snack. It's a homey-style sandwich, and the dumpling is homey, too. There's no red sauce in this dumpling, but the salami is the most Italian–American thing ever. These are a little spicy. The mustard is the traditional accompaniment for maximum enjoyment.

In a small bowl, combine the salami, provolone, Parmesan, bok choy and scallions. Mix together the mustard and mayo and add to the salami mixture. Season with the pepper and set the mixture aside to let the flavors meld.

Fill a small bowl with water and set aside.

Lay a wonton dough square on a clean work surface at an angle, so that it looks like a diamond. Place 1 heaping teaspoon of the salami filling in the center of the wonton square. Wet your fingers in the small bowl of water and run a damp finger along all four outside edges of the wrapper.

Carefully pick up the wonton skin and lay it in the palm of your hand, keeping the points pointing up toward your middle finger and down to the base of your palm. Gently fold the bottom point of the skin up over the filling, creating a triangle, then gently press the seams to close them well. Using the tip of your finger, wet the two diagonal sides and begin sealing the seam on the left side making small folds from the left side slightly over the right (similar to crimping a pie crust). Remember to line up the edges of the wrapper as you pleat and press all the way around. Continue pleating seven to ten times until the dumpling is completely sealed. The finished dumpling will have a half-moon shape. (See more on page 58.) Place the finished dumpling on a sheet pan and cover with a tea towel or damp paper towel to keep them moist while working. Continue making dumplings until you have used all the filling and wrappers.

Place a large sauté pan with a tight-fitting lid over medium–high heat. Add 1 to 2 tablespoons (15 to 30 ml) of the soybean oil to the pan and heat to a shimmer, 3 to 4 minutes. Add six to eight dumplings to the pan at a time to prevent crowding and cook for 4 to 5 minutes, until the bottoms of the dumplings are brown and crispy. Carefully pour ¼ cup (60 ml) of water into the pan and cover the pan with a lid. Let the dumplings steam for 3 to 4 minutes, until the filling is cooked through and the skin has formed a tight seal (the dumplings should lift easily from the bottom of the pan). Cook the rest of the dumplings in batches of six to eight, adding more oil as necessary.

Serve immediately with mustard for dipping.

Chicken Dumplings

Sesame Ginger Chicken Wontons

YIELD: 24 DUMPLINGS

1 lb (454 g) ground chicken

4 cloves garlic, minced

4 tsp (8 g) fresh ginger, minced

3 tbsp (45 ml) soy sauce

2 tsp (10 ml) rice vinegar

3 tbsp (45 ml) sesame oil

3 scallions, sliced thin

24 wonton wrappers, rolled thin

3–4 tbsp (45–60 ml) soybean oil

Sesame Ginger Chicken Wontons are a house specialty—these are a fusion dumpling that uses Asian ingredients, but they were created for Brooklyn Chop House. They take advantage of a super-simple blend of the Asian flavors of ginger, garlic and soy, and they are just plain tasty! These are very popular with regulars, and excellent for those who don't eat red meat. These are so easy—probably among the easiest to make in the book—which also makes them perfect for getting kids involved with cooking.

Combine the ground chicken, garlic, ginger, soy sauce, rice vinegar, sesame oil and scallions in a small bowl; let the mixture sit for 10 minutes.

Fill a small bowl with water and set aside.

Lay a wonton dough square on a clean work surface at an angle, so that it looks like a diamond. Place 1 heaping tablespoon (15 g) of the chicken mixture in the middle of the wrapper. Wet your fingers in the small bowl of water and run a damp finger along all four outside edges of the wrapper, then lift it into the palm of your hand. Fold the bottom point up to the top and seal the wonton, pressing out the excess air. You should now have a triangle. Wet the bottom points and fold them in on each other to create a tortellini-shaped wonton (see more on page 54).

Place a large sauté pan with a tight-fitting lid over medium–high heat. Add 1 to 2 tablespoons (15 to 30 ml) of the soybean oil to the pan and heat to a shimmer, 3 to 4 minutes. Add six to eight dumplings to the pan at a time to prevent crowding and cook for 4 to 5 minutes, until the bottoms of the dumplings are brown and crispy. Carefully pour ¼ cup (60 ml) of water into the pan and cover the pan with a lid. Let the dumplings steam for 3 to 4 minutes, until the filling is cooked through and the skin has formed a tight seal (the dumplings should lift easily from the bottom of the pan). Cook the rest of the dumplings in batches of six to eight, adding more oil as necessary. Serve immediately.

Chicken Parmigiana Dumplings

I love chicken parmigiana so much I could eat it for breakfast, lunch and dinner. It's just the ultimate comfort food to me. You can tell a New York kid by how devoted to their red sauce they are. Pizza, chicken parm, pasta—I love it all. This classic dish works perfectly as a dumpling, with the wrapper mimicking pasta, the traditional side for chicken parmigiana. The marinara dipping sauce is, like, twelve times better than anything you buy, and super easy. I totally recommend trying it—you can use store bought instead, but this is so easy to make.

Preheat the oven to 375°F (190°C). Line a sheet pan with parchment paper and set aside.

Set up a breading station as follows: put the flour in one shallow bowl; beat the egg, water, salt, pepper and minced garlic in a second shallow bowl; and mix the breadcrumbs, parsley and Parmesan cheese in a third shallow bowl. Set one more plate or shallow bowl out to hold the finished chicken. Take the first piece of chicken and lay it in the flour, flipping to coat it completely. Shake off the excess flour and lay the chicken into the egg mixture, flipping to coat completely. Shake off the excess egg mixture and then lay the chicken into the breadcrumb mixture, flipping to make sure it's coated evenly. Place the breadcrumb-coated chicken on the empty plate and continue with the remaining chicken. Let the chicken rest at least 20 minutes, so that the egg can dry slightly and adhere the coating to the chicken.

Place a large sauté pan over medium–high heat, add ½ cup (120 ml) of the vegetable oil and heat until the oil begins to shimmer. Carefully place two to three pieces of breadcrumb-coated chicken at a time into the pan and cook for 5 to 6 minutes per side, until lightly browned and crispy. Place the chicken onto the parchment-lined sheet pan and continue with the remaining chicken. Place the tray of browned chicken into the preheated oven and bake for 10 to 12 minutes, until the chicken is cooked through. Let the chicken cool then roughly chop. Set aside.

To make the marinara dipping sauce, place a small pan over medium heat and warm the olive oil until it begins to shimmer. Add the chopped onion, garlic, dried oregano and dried basil. Cook for 6 to 8 minutes, until the onion is translucent. Add the crushed tomatoes and season with salt and pepper, stir well and simmer for 15 to 20 minutes until slightly thickened. Set aside for dipping.

Fill a small bowl with water and set aside.

(continued)

YIELD: 24 DUMPLINGS

DUMPLINGS

1 cup (125 g) all-purpose flour

1 egg

3 tbsp (45 ml) water

½ tsp kosher salt

½ tsp black pepper

2 cloves garlic, minced

1 cup (125 g) breadcrumbs

2 tbsp (8 g) chopped parsley

¼ cup (20 g) grated Parmesan cheese

1 lb (454 g) chicken breast, boneless and skinless (sliced in half lengthwise if thicker than ½ inch [13 mm])

2½ cups (600 ml) vegetable oil, divided

24 circular wonton wrappers, rolled thick

4 oz (113 g) mozzarella cheese, chopped

MARINARA DIPPING SAUCE

2 tbsp (30 ml) olive oil

½ onion, chopped

2–3 cloves garlic, minced

2 tsp (2 g) dried oregano

2 tsp (2 g) dried basil

1 (14-oz [397-g]) can crushed tomatoes

Kosher salt

Black pepper

Chicken Parmigiana Dumplings (cont.)

Place a wonton wrapper on a clean surface. Place 1 tablespoon (15 g) of the chopped fried chicken pieces in the center of each wrapper, and top with a bit of the chopped mozzarella. Dip your fingers in the small bowl of water and using a damp finger, wet the outer edges. Bring the left-hand top and bottom points together and squeeze to seal. Bring the right-hand point up to meet the first points and squeeze all the seams tightly to make sure the dumpling is sealed into a 3D triangle shape (see more on page 57). Place the finished dumplings on a sheet pan and cover with a towel. Repeat with the remaining wonton wrappers and filling.

Place a large deep pot over medium–high heat and add the remaining 2 cups (480 ml) of the vegetable oil. Heat the oil to 365°F (185°C). Line a sheet pan with paper towels for draining. Carefully lower six dumplings at a time into the hot oil (don't add more than six at a time, or it will lower the temperature of the oil too fast and your dumplings will be greasy instead of crispy). Move the dumplings around with a metal spoon so they don't stick to each other, and fry for 5 to 6 minutes until well browned and crispy. Drain the dumplings on the paper towel–lined sheet pan and repeat with the remaining dumplings.

Serve hot with warm marinara dipping sauce.

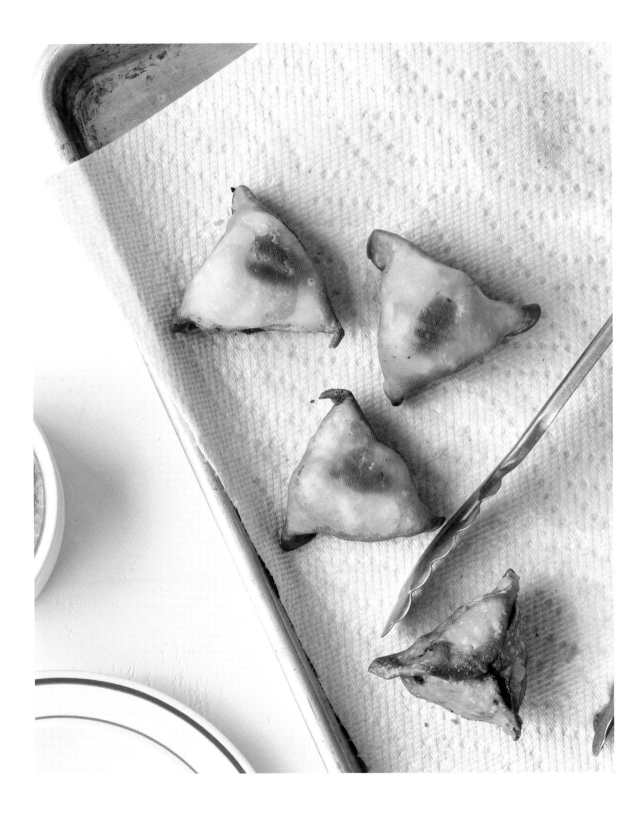

Fried Chicken Dumplings

Chick-fil-A® has nothing on us! We are putting a little spin on a fried chicken sandwich with these dumplings. The dough stands in for the bread, and honey mustard is the go-to sauce. These are pretty kid friendly, and you can play with the sauces—I also like BBQ with these dumplings. These are also fun for the 4th of July, or for a picnic. These are also great for a dumpling party where you make an assortment of dumplings to serve—these would be great paired with the Bacon Cheeseburger Shumai (page 24), for example. Be careful not to overcook these, so you don't lose the crunch of the crispy chicken. Deeelish!

Place the soybean oil in a deep heavy pot and bring the oil up to 360°F (180°C). Set paper towels on a sheet pan for draining the chicken.

In a large bowl, combine the flour, salt, pepper, garlic powder, onion powder and cayenne and mix well. Divide the flour mixture evenly into two bowls. Add the cut-up chicken to one bowl of the flour mixture and toss to evenly coat all the chicken with the flour mixture. Slowly pour the beer into the second bowl of flour mixture and stir to create a batter (it will bubble up, so don't pour too fast!).

When the oil is up to temperature, pull a piece of chicken from the seasoned flour and shake it well to remove any excess flour. Add the chicken to the beer batter and coat well. Remove from the batter and shake gently to remove any excess batter. Gently place the battered chicken, six to eight pieces at a time, into the hot oil (do not drop them in as the hot oil will splatter and burn you!). Using a metal spoon, gently move the chicken pieces around in the hot oil so that they don't stick together. Fry each batch for 4 to 6 minutes until the chicken is golden brown and cooked through. Remove the fried chicken from the oil and drain on the paper towel–lined sheet pan. Season the drained chicken with a few shakes of kosher salt. Repeat with the remaining chicken pieces and let the chicken cool slightly. When cool enough to handle, give the chicken pieces a rough chop, being careful to keep as much crispy texture intact as possible.

Fill a small bowl with water and set aside. Line a sheet pan with parchment paper and set aside.

Place a wonton dough square on a clean work surface at an angle, so that it looks like a diamond. Place approximately 1 tablespoon (15 g) of chopped fried chicken pieces in the center of the square. Top with a bit of honey mustard and a few scallions. Wet your fingers in the small bowl of water and run a damp finger along all four outside edges of the wrapper, then carefully pull together the top and bottom points and press to seal. Pull the two side points to the center of the dumpling and seal the sides to create a pyramid shape (see more on page 31). Place the finished dumpling on a parchment-lined sheet pan and cover with a towel. Repeat with the remaining wonton squares and filling.

Place the dumplings into a steamer basket and set over a pot of simmering water. Cover with a lid and steam gently for 5 to 6 minutes, until the wonton skins are translucent and the filling is warmed through. Serve with extra honey mustard for dipping.

YIELD: 24 DUMPLINGS

2 cups (480 ml) soybean oil

2 cups (250 g) all-purpose flour

6 tsp (30 g) kosher salt, plus more to taste

4 tsp (8 g) black pepper

3 tsp (8 g) garlic powder

2 tsp (3 g) onion powder

1 tsp cayenne

2 lbs (908 g) chicken breasts, cut into 1-inch (3-cm) pieces

4 oz (120 ml) Guinness or dark lager of choice

24 wonton wrappers, rolled thick

½ cup (120 ml) honey mustard, plus more for dipping

2 scallions, thinly sliced

Seafood & Fish Dumplings

Rock & Lobster Roll Dumplings

YIELD: 24 DUMPLINGS

1½ lbs (680 g) lobster meat (claws, knuckles and tails) steamed, chilled and chopped

⅓ cup (35 g) celery, diced

4 tbsp (56 g) butter, melted and cooled

Juice of 1 lemon

1 tsp smoked paprika

½ tsp kosher salt

¼ tsp black pepper

4 leaves of Romaine lettuce, finely shredded

24 wonton wrappers, rolled thin

½ cup (120 ml) soybean oil

Pickle chips, for garnish

Black sesame seeds, for garnish

In the United States, each region prepares their lobster rolls differently . . . some use mayo, some butter, some are simply seasoned with salt and pepper, some use Old Bay seasoning. I personally like mine dressed with butter, on a split hot dog bun, which is really similar to the Connecticut style. Our dumpling version is simple, and the butter just binds the lobster, while the celery adds a little snap. You can serve these with potato chips, and a coke, if you like. This is another great recipe for a 4th of July celebration. Very decadent!

In a large bowl, combine the lobster meat, celery, butter, lemon juice, smoked paprika, salt, pepper and shredded lettuce, and toss well to combine.

Fill a small bowl with water and set aside.

Lay a wonton dough square on a clean work surface at an angle, so that it looks like a diamond. Place 1 heaping teaspoon of the lobster filling in the center of the wonton square. Wet your fingers in the small bowl of water and run a damp finger along all four outside edges of the wrapper.

Carefully pick up the wonton skin and lay it in the palm of your hand, keeping the points pointing up toward your middle finger and down to the base of your palm. Gently fold the bottom point of the skin up over the filling, creating a triangle, then gently press the seams to close them well. Using the tip of your finger, wet the two diagonal sides and begin sealing the seam on the left side making small folds from the left side slightly over the right (similar to crimping a pie crust). Remember to line up the edges of the wrapper as you pleat and press all the way around. Continue pleating seven to ten times until the dumpling is completely sealed. The finished dumpling will have a half-moon shape. (See more on page 58.) Place the finished dumpling on a sheet pan and cover with a tea towel or damp paper towel to keep them moist while working. Continue making dumplings until you have used all the filling and wrappers.

Place a large pan with a tight-fitting lid over high heat, and add 1–2 tablespoons (15–30 ml) of the oil. Lay six to eight wontons at a time in the hot oil and let cook for 2 to 3 minutes. Add ¼ cup (60 ml) of water to the pan and cover with the lid. Let the dumplings steam for 3 to 4 minutes, until the skins are translucent.

Serve immediately, garnished with pickle chips and black sesame seeds.

Shrimp & Scallion Dumplings

These are delicious! Shrimp flavored with ginger is a zingy, yet refreshing, flavor profile, and it's great that the filling is actually very simple. Dumplings are traditional for Chinese New Year and symbolize family togetherness. I could see these as a great hors d'oeuvre for the winter holidays, especially when paired with any of our vegetable dumplings (see pages 94–103), or maybe with the Green Shrimp & Mushroom Dumplings (page 80).

YIELD: 24 DUMPLINGS

1½ lbs (680 g) shrimp, peeled, deveined and finely chopped

3 tbsp (45 ml) vegetable oil

2–3 cloves garlic, minced

1 tbsp (6 g) fresh ginger, peeled and minced

2 tsp (10 ml) soy sauce

3 large scallions, chopped

¼ tsp kosher salt

24 wonton wrappers, rolled thin

Asian-style hot mustard and soy sauce, for dipping

In a medium bowl, combine the shrimp, oil, garlic, ginger, soy sauce, scallions and salt, and stir well to combine.

Fill a small bowl with water and set aside.

Lay a wonton dough square on a clean work surface at an angle, so that it looks like a diamond. Place 1 heaping teaspoon of the shrimp filling in the center of the wonton square. Wet your fingers in the small bowl of water and run a damp finger along all four outside edges of the wrapper.

Carefully pick up the wonton skin and lay it in the palm of your hand, keeping the points pointing up toward your middle finger and down to the base of your palm. Gently fold the bottom point of the skin up over the filling, creating a triangle, then gently press the seams to close them well. Using the tip of your finger, wet the two diagonal sides and begin sealing the seam on the left side making small folds from the left side slightly over the right (similar to crimping a pie crust). Remember to line up the edges of the wrapper as you pleat and press all the way around. Continue pleating seven to ten times until the dumpling is completely sealed. The finished dumpling will have a half-moon shape. (See more on page 58.) Place the finished dumpling on a sheet pan and cover with a tea towel or damp paper towel to keep them moist while working. Continue making dumplings until you have used all the filling and wrappers.

Place the dumplings into a steamer basket and set over a pot of simmering water. Cover with a lid and steam gently for 5 to 6 minutes, until the wonton skins are translucent and the filling is warmed through.

Serve with hot mustard and soy sauce for dipping.

Green Shrimp & Mushroom Dumplings

YIELD: 24 DUMPLINGS

6 jumbo shrimp, peeled and deveined

2 tbsp (30 ml) olive oil

2 cups (145 g) cremini mushrooms, cleaned and thinly sliced

1 cup (70 g) shiitake mushrooms, woody stems removed, cleaned and thinly sliced

2 tbsp (30 ml) dry sherry

6 oz (170 g) medium shrimp, peeled and deveined

5 scallions, ends removed and thinly sliced

3 tbsp (45 ml) soy sauce

2 tsp (4 g) fresh ginger, peeled and chopped

1 tbsp (15 ml) toasted sesame oil

24 wonton wrappers, rolled thin

4–6 large cabbage leaves

Sambal oelek, for serving

These are truly exotic and very impressive. They use a touch of sambal oelek, which is a chili paste, for heat, but you can easily use Sriracha, which may be easier to find—the important aspect is the chili. These also use an unusual technique in which the filling is chopped finely, but mixed with the larger shrimp for texture. Bubba from Forrest Gump would love these.

Carefully slice each of the jumbo shrimp in half lengthwise, then cut each half in half crosswise (you will end up with 24 pieces of shrimp). Set aside.

Place a large sauté pan over medium–high heat. Add the olive oil and heat until the oil begins to shimmer. Add the cremini and shiitake mushrooms and let them cook for 8 to 10 minutes, without stirring, until they become deeply browned on the bottom. Toss and cook for another 4 to 5 minutes, until the mushrooms are cooked through. Add the sherry to the pan and cook for 2 to 3 more minutes, until the liquid has evaporated. Remove the cooked mushrooms from the pan and place them in the bowl of a food processor. Add the medium shrimp (not the ones that you already cut up), scallions, soy sauce, ginger and sesame oil. Pulse the food processor ten to fifteen times until the mixture is finely chopped, but not a paste.

Fill a small bowl with water and set aside.

Lay a wonton dough square on a clean work surface at an angle, so that it looks like a diamond. Place 1 heaping teaspoon of the shrimp and mushroom filling in the center of the wonton square. Place one of the jumbo shrimp quarters on top. Wet your fingers in the small bowl of water and run a damp finger along all four outside edges of the wrapper.

Carefully pick up the wonton skin and lay it in the palm of your hand, keeping the points pointing up toward your middle finger and down to the base of your palm. Gently fold the bottom point of the skin up over the filling, creating a triangle, then gently press the seams to close them well. Using the tip of your finger, wet the two diagonal sides and begin sealing the seam on the left side making small folds from the left side slightly over the right (similar to crimping a pie crust). Remember to line up the edges of the wrapper as you pleat and press all the way around. Continue pleating seven to ten times until the dumpling is completely sealed. The finished dumpling will have a half-moon shape. (See more on page 58.) Place the finished dumpling on a sheet pan and cover with a tea towel or damp paper towel to keep them moist while working. Continue making dumplings until you have used all the filling and wrappers.

Place the cabbage leaves into the bottom of a steamer basket, then lay the dumplings on top of the leaves. Place the steamer basket over a pot of simmering water. Cover with the lid and steam gently for 10 to 12 minutes, until the wonton skins are translucent and the filling is cooked through. Discard the cabbage leaves, and garnish the dumplings with a drop of sambal oelek to serve.

Cod & Chive Dumplings

These are fancy, with a capital F! You can use black bass in this recipe, as we do at Brooklyn Chop House, but it is very expensive, and the recipe works well with cod. This recipe harkens back to 1960s canapes with the filling—it's like a refined fish mousse. These would be amazing as a formal appetizer.

In a medium bowl, combine the cod, salt, pepper, chicken stock, soy sauce, rice wine and sesame oil. Toss to combine. Transfer the mixture to the bowl of a food processor. Pulse the fish mixture twelve to fifteen times, until a coarse paste forms, stopping to scrape down the sides of the bowl when needed. Return the paste to the medium bowl and add the ginger and scallions, stirring well to combine. Cover with plastic wrap and let sit for at least 30 minutes for the flavors to meld. (You can also refrigerate overnight, but be sure you bring the mixture back to room temperature before forming the dumplings.)

Fill a small bowl with water and set aside.

Lay a wonton dough square on a clean work surface at an angle, so that it looks like a diamond. Place 1 heaping teaspoon of the cod filling in the center of the wonton square. Wet your fingers in the small bowl of water and run a damp finger along all four outside edges of the wrapper.

Carefully pick up the wonton skin and lay it in the palm of your hand, keeping the points pointing up toward your middle finger and down to the base of your palm. Gently fold the bottom point of the skin up over the filling, creating a triangle, then gently press the seams to close them well. Using the tip of your finger, wet the two diagonal sides and begin sealing the seam on the left side making small folds from the left side slightly over the right (similar to crimping a pie crust). Remember to line up the edges of the wrapper as you pleat and press all the way around. Continue pleating seven to ten times until the dumpling is completely sealed. The finished dumpling will have a half-moon shape. (See more on page 58.) Place the finished dumpling on a sheet pan and cover with a tea towel or damp paper towel to keep them moist while working. Continue making dumplings until you have used all the filling and wrappers.

Place eight to ten dumplings into a steamer basket and set over a pot of simmering water. Cover with a lid and steam gently for 10 to 12 minutes, until the filling is cooked through and the skins are tightly formed around the filling. Remove the dumplings from the basket and continue steaming in batches.

Serve with extra soy sauce for dipping.

1½ lbs (680 g) cod, patted dry and cut into 1-inch (3-cm) pieces

½ tsp kosher salt

¼ tsp white pepper (or black pepper)

¼ cup (60 ml) chicken stock

1½ tbsp (23 ml) soy sauce, plus extra for dipping

1 tbsp (15 ml) shaoxing rice wine or seasoned rice wine vinegar

2 tbsp (30 ml) sesame oil

1½ tbsp (9 g) fresh ginger, peeled and minced

3 scallions, ends trimmed and sliced thin

24 wonton wrappers, rolled thick

Spicy Chili Seafood Dumplings

YIELD: 24 DUMPLINGS

1 lb (454 g) cooked crabmeat, finely chopped (or 10 oz [284 g] imitation crabmeat, finely chopped)

4 oz (114 g) cooked shrimp, finely chopped

1 stick celery, sliced into long strips then finely diced

1 small carrot, peeled and finely diced

¼ cup (4 g) cilantro, chopped

¼ cup (55 g) mayonnaise

½ tsp kosher salt

¼ tsp black pepper

24 wonton wrappers, rolled thick

XO sauce or another sauce, for dipping

Every holiday season, we focus on seafood for our Christmas Eve feast. These are a succulent version of a seafood dumpling invented for Brooklyn Chop House. XO sauce is a Chinese staple. You don't have to use it though—Sriracha is also good, and may be easier to find. Plum sauce is another option. It is sweet, and always a fan fave. You can serve these dumplings with any of the above options— or play around and find or make your own favorite dipping sauce to pair with these dumplings.

In a medium bowl, combine the crabmeat, shrimp, celery, carrot, cilantro, mayonnaise, salt and pepper. Mix well, then taste and adjust the seasonings if needed.

Fill a small bowl with water and set aside.

Lay a wonton dough square on a clean work surface at an angle, so that it looks like a diamond. Place 1 heaping teaspoon of the seafood filling in the center of the wonton square. Wet your fingers in the small bowl of water and run a damp finger along all four outside edges of the wrapper.

Carefully pick up the wonton skin and lay it in the palm of your hand, keeping the points pointing up toward your middle finger and down to the base of your palm. Gently fold the bottom point of the skin up over the filling, creating a triangle, then gently press the seams to close them well. Using the tip of your finger, wet the two diagonal sides and begin sealing the seam on the left side making small folds from the left side slightly over the right (similar to crimping a pie crust). Remember to line up the edges of the wrapper as you pleat and press all the way around. Continue pleating seven to ten times until the dumpling is completely sealed. The finished dumpling will have a half-moon shape. (See more on page 58.) Place the finished dumpling on a sheet pan and cover with a tea towel or damp paper towel to keep them moist while working. Continue making dumplings until you have used all the filling and wrappers.

Place eight to ten dumplings into a steamer basket and set over a pot of simmering water. Cover with a lid and steam gently for 10 to 12 minutes, until the filling is cooked through and the skins are tightly formed around the filling. Remove the dumplings from the basket and continue steaming in batches.

Serve with XO sauce or another sauce for dipping.

Crab & Spinach Dumplings

These crab and spinach dumplings are a light bite. The beurre blanc sauce is a light white wine sauce, and is traditionally paired with fish. It is sometimes used instead of hollandaise—it's actually a little lighter and brighter and it really elevates this dumpling. This recipe is what I call a "fancy" dumpling and these could easily pair with champagne. You can use king crab in this recipe to really make it special.

YIELD: 24 DUMPLINGS

DUMPLINGS

1 lb (454 g) fresh spinach, stems removed and rinsed to remove any dirt

1½ lbs (680 g) crabmeat, picked through to remove all bits of shell and cartilage

1 large egg, lightly beaten

2 tbsp (16 g) all-purpose flour

¼ tsp cayenne

¼ tsp ground nutmeg

⅛ tsp black pepper

¼ tsp kosher salt

24 wonton wrappers, rolled thick

1 cup (240 ml) soybean oil

BEURRE BLANC

1 cup (240 ml) dry white wine

1½ sticks (12 oz [340 g]) unsalted butter, cubed and frozen

Juice of 1 lemon

1 tbsp (4 g) flat-leaf parsley, chopped

¼ tsp kosher salt

Black pepper, to taste

Bring a large pot of salted water to a boil. Fill a large bowl with ice water and lay out paper towels on a sheet pan. Add the spinach to the boiling water and cook for 1 minute until just tender and still bright green. Remove the spinach from the boiling water and place it in the ice water to shock it. Move the spinach to the paper towels and let it drain for a few minutes. Using your hands, squeeze out all the excess water from the cooled spinach, then give it a rough chop.

In a medium bowl, combine the blanched and chopped spinach, crabmeat, egg, flour, cayenne, nutmeg, pepper and salt.

Fill a small bowl with water and set aside.

Lay a wonton dough square on a clean work surface at an angle, so that it looks like a diamond. Place 1 heaping teaspoon of the crab filling in the center of the wonton square. Wet your fingers in the small bowl of water and run a damp finger along all four outside edges of the wrapper.

Carefully pick up the wonton skin and lay it in the palm of your hand, keeping the points pointing up toward your middle finger and down to the base of your palm. Gently fold the bottom point of the skin up over the filling, creating a triangle, then gently press the seams to close them well. Using the tip of your finger, wet the two diagonal sides and begin sealing the seam on the left side making small folds from the left side slightly over the right (similar to crimping a pie crust). Remember to line up the edges of the wrapper as you pleat and press all the way around. Continue pleating seven to ten times until the dumpling is completely sealed. The finished dumpling will have a half-moon shape. (See more on page 58.) Place the finished dumpling on a sheet pan and cover with a tea towel or damp paper towel to keep them moist while working. Continue making dumplings until you have used all the filling and wrappers.

To make the buerre blanc sauce, pour the wine into a small heavy-bottomed saucepan, bring it to a simmer and cook until reduced to approximately 2 to 3 tablespoons (30 to 45 ml). Slowly whisk in the cold butter, a few cubes at a time, waiting to add more butter until the previous cubes are completely melted and incorporated. When all the butter is melted, add the lemon juice and parsley, then season with salt and pepper. Leave the saucepan over low heat to keep the sauce warm while you fry the dumplings.

Place the soybean oil into a large sauté pan and heat until the oil shimmers. Place six to eight dumplings in the hot oil and fry for 4 to 5 minutes on each side, until lightly browned and crispy. Continue with the rest of the dumplings.

Serve immediately with the warm beurre blanc.

Scallop & Shrimp Dumplings

YIELD: 24 DUMPLINGS

DUMPLINGS

1 lb (454 g) large scallops (or bay scallops), minced

8 oz (227 g) raw shrimp, peeled, deveined and roughly chopped

3–4 scallions, ends trimmed and sliced thin

4 cloves garlic, minced

1 tbsp (6 g) fresh ginger, peeled and minced

4 tbsp (60 ml) soy sauce

4 tbsp (60 ml) sesame oil

¼ tsp kosher salt

¼ tsp black pepper

24 wonton wrappers, rolled thin

3–4 tbsp (45–60 ml) soybean oil

DIPPING SAUCE

¼ cup (60 ml) soy sauce

¼ tsp chili flakes

These briny beauties are little delicate puffs of a dumpling. They are about as dainty as it gets, and are divine with white wine. I personally prefer a Sauvignon blanc. I think a dumpling party featuring all of the seafood dumplings would be a fantastic dinner party theme. As with all the fish and seafood dumplings, be careful not to overcook.

In a medium bowl, combine the scallops, shrimp, scallions, garlic, ginger, soy sauce, sesame oil, salt and pepper. Let the mixture chill for 20 minutes to allow the flavors to meld.

To make the dipping sauce, mix the soy sauce and chili flakes in a small bowl; set aside.

Fill a small bowl with water and set aside. Line a sheet pan with parchment paper.

Lay out a wonton square with the points pointing up and down. Place 1 tablespoon (15 g) of the chilled seafood filling in the center of the square. Wet your fingers in the small bowl of water and run a damp finger along all four outside edges of the wrapper, then lift it into the palm of your hand. Fold the bottom point up to the top and seal the wonton, pressing out the excess air. You should now have a triangle. Wet the bottom points and fold them in on each other to create a tortellini-shaped wonton (see more on page 54). Place the finished dumplings on the parchment-lined sheet pan and cover with a towel. Repeat with the remaining wonton squares and filling.

Place a large sauté pan with a tight-fitting lid over medium–high heat. Add 1–2 tablespoons (15–30 ml) of soybean oil to the pan and heat until the oil starts to shimmer. Add six to eight dumplings to the pan at a time to prevent crowding and cook for 4 to 5 minutes, until the bottoms of the dumplings are brown and crispy. Carefully pour ¼ cup (60 ml) of water into the pan and cover the pan with a lid. Let the dumplings steam for 3 to 4 minutes, until the filling is cooked through and the skin has formed a tight seal (the dumplings should lift easily from the bottom of the pan). Cook the rest of the dumplings in batches of six to eight, adding more oil as necessary.

Serve immediately with the dipping sauce.

Gluten-Free Pork & Shrimp Dumplings

These are Chinese dumplings all the way. The spices are designed to bring out the flavors and textures for an optimum dumpling experience, but without wheat. You can omit the sambal oelek and use Sriracha, which can be found in any grocery store. I like the sambal oelek, though—its heat is welcome, and it tastes a little more exotic.

In a medium bowl, toss the cabbage with the salt and set aside for 30 minutes to shed moisture. Then, place the cabbage in a clean kitchen towel and wring it out to extract as much liquid as possible. Spread the cabbage onto paper towels to dry completely.

In a large bowl, combine the cabbage with the pork, shrimp, scallions, garlic, shaoxing, ginger, soy sauce, sesame oil, sugar and pepper. Stir until well mixed. Refrigerate for at least 20 minutes.

To make the dipping sauce, combine the soy sauce, sesame oil and sambal oelek in a small bowl; set aside. Fill a small bowl with water and set aside.

Lay a wonton dough square on a clean work surface at an angle, so that it looks like a diamond. Place 1 heaping teaspoon of the seafood filling in the center of the wonton square. Wet your fingers in the small bowl of water and run a damp finger along all four outside edges of the wrapper.

Carefully pick up the wonton skin and lay it in the palm of your hand, keeping the points pointing up toward your middle finger and down to the base of your palm. Gently fold the bottom point of the skin up over the filling, creating a triangle, then gently press the seams to close them well. Using the tip of your finger, wet the two diagonal sides and begin sealing the seam on the left side making small folds from the left side slightly over the right (similar to crimping a pie crust). Remember to line up the edges of the wrapper as you pleat and press all the way around. Continue pleating seven to ten times until the dumpling is completely sealed. The finished dumpling will have a half-moon shape. (See more on page 58.) Place the finished dumpling on a sheet pan and cover with a tea towel or damp paper towel to keep them moist while working. Continue making dumplings until you have used all the filling and wrappers.

Place a large sauté pan with a tight-fitting lid over medium–high heat. Add 1 to 2 tablespoons (15 to 30 ml) of the soybean oil to the pan and heat to a shimmer, 3 to 4 minutes. Add six to eight dumplings to the pan at a time to prevent crowding and cook for 4 to 5 minutes, until the bottoms of the dumplings are brown and crispy. Carefully pour ¼ cup (60 ml) of water into the pan and cover the pan with a lid. Let the dumplings steam for 3 to 4 minutes, until the filling is cooked through and the skin has formed a tight seal (the dumplings should lift easily from the bottom of the pan). Cook the rest of the dumplings in batches of six to eight, adding more oil as necessary.

Garnish with sesame seeds and serve immediately with the dipping sauce.

YIELD: 24 DUMPLINGS

DUMPLINGS

2 cups (140 g) Napa cabbage, shredded

2 tsp (12 g) kosher salt

1 lb (454 g) ground pork

8 oz (227 g) peeled, deveined shrimp, coarsely chopped

3 medium scallions, thinly sliced

3 large cloves garlic, minced

2 tbsp (30 ml) shaoxing (Chinese rice wine) or dry sherry

1½ tbsp (9 g) grated fresh ginger

1 tbsp (15 ml) soy sauce

2 tsp (10 ml) toasted sesame oil

½ tsp granulated sugar

¼ tsp freshly ground black pepper

24 gluten-free wonton wrappers, rolled thick

3–4 tbsp (45–60 ml) soybean oil, divided

Sesame seeds, for garnish

DIPPING SAUCE

¼ cup (60 ml) soy sauce

1 tsp sesame oil

1 tsp sambal oelek

Lobster Crunch Dumplings

YIELD: 24 DUMPLINGS

8 oz (227 g) cream cheese, softened

1 lb (454 g) lobster meat, steamed, removed from shell and chopped (or 2 [6.5-oz (184-g)] cans lobster meat, drained, picked though for shells and chopped)

4 scallions, sliced thin

1 tbsp (15 ml) soy sauce

1 tsp rice wine vinegar

¼ tsp black pepper

Salt, to taste

24 wonton wrappers, rolled thin

4 cups (960 ml) soybean oil

If you like crab rangoon, you will love these. They are a creamy lobster dumpling fried and served hot. The lobster meat preferably comes from fresh lobster, but you can substitute canned if you like. In general, I prefer to use all fresh ingredients, like we use at Brooklyn Chop House. Lobster is actually super easy to steam or boil, and it takes very little time. Crab can also be substituted for lobster to make crab rangoon dumplings.

In a medium bowl, gently fold together the cream cheese, lobster, scallions, soy sauce, rice wine vinegar and pepper; season to taste with salt if needed.

Fill a small bowl with water and set aside.

Lay a wonton dough square on a clean work surface at an angle, so that it looks like a diamond. Place 1 heaping teaspoon of the lobster filling in the center of the wonton square. Wet your fingers in the small bowl of water and run a damp finger along all four outside edges of the wrapper.

Carefully pick up the wonton skin and lay it in the palm of your hand, keeping the points pointing up toward your middle finger and down to the base of your palm. Gently fold the bottom point of the skin up over the filling, creating a triangle, then gently press the seams to close them well. Using the tip of your finger, wet the two diagonal sides and begin sealing the seam on the left side making small folds from the left side slightly over the right (similar to crimping a pie crust). Remember to line up the edges of the wrapper as you pleat and press all the way around. Continue pleating seven to ten times until the dumpling is completely sealed. The finished dumpling will have a half-moon shape. (See more on page 58.) Place the finished dumpling on a sheet pan and cover with a tea towel or damp paper towel to keep them moist while working. Continue making dumplings until you have used all the filling and wrappers.

Place a deep heavy pan over medium–high heat and add the oil and heat until the oil begins to shimmer. Carefully place six to eight dumplings in the hot oil (frying too many wontons at once will lower the temperature of the oil too fast, and your wontons will be greasy instead of crispy). Let the dumplings fry for 4 to 5 minutes, until lightly browned and crispy. Drain on paper towels and repeat with the rest of the dumplings.

Serve immediately.

Vegetable Dumplings

Edamame Truffle Dumplings

YIELD: 24 DUMPLINGS

Taking this staple Asian soybean to the next level, this dumpling is as tasty as it is light. These dumplings are filled with a creamy edamame-truffle purée, wrapped in a tender wonton wrapper and doused in a shallot–Sauternes broth. These are perfect as an appetizer or just as a snack.

DUMPLINGS

3 cups (465 g) edamame, steamed and shelled (if frozen, defrost fully before using)

¼ lb (113 g) unsalted butter, softened

¼ cup (60 ml) heavy cream

4–5 tbsp (60–75 ml) white truffle oil (or 4 tbsp [56 g] of white truffle butter; if so, decrease the unsalted butter above by an equal amount)

¼ tsp kosher salt, plus more to taste

¼ tsp black pepper, plus more to taste

24 gluten-free wonton wrappers, rolled thin

Chopped chives for garnish

SHALLOT AND SAUTERNES BROTH

2 tbsp (30 ml) soybean oil

¾ cup (120 g) shallots, finely minced

¼ cup (60 ml) Sauternes (or other sweet white wine, such as a white Moscato or sweet Riesling)

¼ cup (60 ml) chicken stock

1 sprig of fresh thyme, leaves picked and chopped

Kosher salt, to taste

Black pepper, to taste

To make the filling, in the bowl of a food processor, combine the edamame, butter, heavy cream, truffle oil, salt and pepper. Pulse the food processor fifteen to twenty times, until the filling is completely smooth with no lumps remaining. Season to taste with more salt and pepper if needed. Refrigerate the filling for at least 4 hours and up to overnight to let it firm up completely.

To make the broth, in a small saucepan over medium heat, heat the oil to a shimmer, then add the shallots. Lower the heat slightly and cook the shallots for 8 to 10 minutes, until they begin to caramelize. Lift the pan off the heat and slowly pour in the wine and then the chicken stock, thyme, salt and pepper. Place the pan back on the heat and deglaze the bottom of the pot, scraping up any brown bits from the bottom. Bring the wine and stock mixture up to boil, then drop to a simmer. Let the liquids simmer and reduce by half. Keep warm until serving time (see Note).

Fill a small bowl with water and set aside.

Lay a wonton dough square on a clean work surface at an angle, so that it looks like a diamond. Place 1 heaping teaspoon of the edamame filling in the center of the wonton square. Wet your fingers in the small bowl of water and run a damp finger along all four outside edges of the wrapper.

Carefully pick up the wonton skin and lay it in the palm of your hand, keeping the points pointing up toward your middle finger and down to the base of your palm. Gently fold the bottom point of the skin up over the filling, creating a triangle, then gently press the seams to close them well. Using the tip of your finger, wet the two diagonal sides and begin sealing the seam on the left side making small folds from the left side slightly over the right (similar to crimping a pie crust). Remember to line up the edges of the wrapper as you pleat and press all the way around. Continue pleating seven to ten times until the dumpling is completely sealed. The finished dumpling will have a half-moon shape. (See more on page 58.) Place the finished dumpling on a sheet pan and cover with a tea towel or damp paper towel to keep them moist while working. Continue making dumplings until you have used all the filling and wrappers.

Place the dumplings into a steamer basket and set over a pot of simmering water. Cover with a lid and steam gently for 10 to 12 minutes, until the filling is cooked through and the skins are tightly formed around the filling. Remove the dumplings from the basket, and spoon the warm broth on top and garnish with chopped chives to serve.

Note: The broth can be made 1 to 2 days ahead of time and stored in the refrigerator. Warm gently in a small saucepan to serve.

"Choy" Slaw Dumplings

The "choy" slaw dumpling is a taste of Asia and it's got a little sweetness to offset the sour. It reminds me a bit of Thai summer rolls, with a peanutty crunch. The sweet and sour flavors meld, and it's an excellent option for vegans—delicious, and just a little exotic. The peanuts add a something something, but you can always leave them out if necessary due to allergies.

These dumplings were the sleeper hit among my cooks. The entire batch disappeared in ten minutes.

YIELD: 24 DUMPLINGS

¼ cup (60 ml) rice vinegar

¼ cup (60 ml) water, for sauce

1 tbsp (12 g) sugar

2 tsp (10 ml) soy sauce, plus more for serving

7 oz (198 g) coleslaw mix (about half a bag)

2 scallions, sliced thin

¼ tsp salt

¼ tsp pepper

Hot sauce, to taste, optional

2 tbsp (18 g) peanuts, finely chopped, optional

24 wonton wrappers, rolled thin

2 tbsp (30 ml) canola or vegetable oil

In a saucepan, combine the vinegar, water, sugar and soy sauce over medium heat until just hot. This will "melt" the sugar into the vinegar, and thicken it slightly, bringing out the flavor of the sauce and softening the sharpness of the vinegar. Add the coleslaw mix to a medium bowl. Pour the vinegar mixture over the coleslaw mix and mix thoroughly. This will "wilt" the coleslaw ever so slightly, making it ready for the dumplings. Add the scallions, salt and pepper and mix thoroughly. Add two splashes of the hot sauce, and/or the peanuts, if using, and mix again.

Fill a small bowl with water and set aside.

Lay a wonton dough square on a clean work surface at an angle, so that it looks like a diamond. Place 1 heaping teaspoon of the coleslaw filling in the center of the wonton square. Wet your fingers in the small bowl of water and run a damp finger along all four outside edges of the wrapper.

Carefully pick up the wonton skin and lay it in the palm of your hand, keeping the points pointing up toward your middle finger and down to the base of your palm. Gently fold the bottom point of the skin up over the filling, creating a triangle, then gently press the seams to close them well. Using the tip of your finger, wet the two diagonal sides and begin sealing the seam on the left side making small folds from the left side slightly over the right (similar to crimping a pie crust). Remember to line up the edges of the wrapper as you pleat and press all the way around. Continue pleating seven to ten times until the dumpling is completely sealed. The finished dumpling will have a half-moon shape. (See more on page 58.) Place the finished dumpling on a sheet pan and cover with a tea towel or damp paper towel to keep them moist while working. Continue making dumplings until you have used all the filling and wrappers.

Heat a 12-inch (30-cm) pan with a tight-fitting lid over high heat. Add the oil to the hot pan, tilting the pan until the bottom is covered with the oil. Wait until you see "waves" in the oil, which means it's hot. Place the dumplings, flat side down, in the hot oil about 2 inches (5 cm) apart, making sure the dumplings don't touch. This should be done in batches of eight, to prevent overcrowding in the pan.

Cook the dumplings for 3 to 4 minutes, until they are nicely browned on the bottom. When the dumplings have browned, carefully pour ¼ cup (60 ml) of water into the pan, and put the lid on. Steam for 4 to 5 minutes, until the dumplings are cooked through.

Serve with soy sauce for dipping.

Tofu & Veggie Dumplings

YIELD: 24 DUMPLINGS

6–7 tbsp (90–105 ml) soybean oil, divided

8 oz (227 g) cremini mushrooms (or white button mushrooms), chopped

½ yellow onion, diced

1 tbsp (6 g) fresh ginger, peeled and minced

2–3 cloves garlic, minced

1 cup (70 g) purple cabbage, finely shredded

½ cup (65 g) carrots, peeled and finely shredded

14 oz (397 g) extra-firm tofu, pressed between paper towels for a few minutes and crumbled

¼ tsp kosher salt

¼ tsp black pepper

2 tbsp (30 ml) soy sauce, plus more for serving

1 tbsp (15 ml) sesame oil

3–4 scallions, thinly sliced

24 wonton wrappers, rolled thin

Everyone needs to eat their veggies. These tofu and veggie dumplings are great to add to the vegan list if made with the gluten-free wonton wrappers. They are also good to pair with the pork dumplings, for a more classic dumpling experience. If people have food allergies, or food restrictions, these are a good bet, and even meat eaters like them.

Place a large sauté pan over medium–high heat. Add 3 tablespoons (45 ml) of the soybean oil and heat until the oil starts to shimmer. Add the mushrooms to the pan and shake the pan until the mushrooms settle into a single layer. Let the mushrooms cook without moving them for 8 to 10 minutes, until the water is released from the mushrooms and begins to evaporate. Add the onion, ginger and garlic. Give the pan a toss and let the vegetables cook for another 6 to 8 minutes, until the onion begins to soften and the ginger and garlic become fragrant but not browned. Add the cabbage to the pan and cook, stirring occasionally, for 5 minutes, or until the cabbage is wilted but still has a bit of crunch to it. Remove the pan from the heat and pour the veggie mixture into a large bowl to cool slightly.

Then add the carrots, tofu, salt, pepper, soy sauce, sesame oil and scallions. Toss well to combine, and taste for seasoning. Let the mixture cool completely.

Lay a wonton dough square on a clean work surface at an angle, so that it looks like a diamond. Place 1 heaping teaspoon of the tofu and veggie filling in the center of the wonton square. Wet your fingers in a small bowl of water and run a damp finger along all four outside edges of the wrapper.

Carefully pick up the wonton skin and lay it in the palm of your hand, keeping the points pointing up toward your middle finger and down to the base of your palm. Gently fold the bottom point of the skin up over the filling, creating a triangle, then gently press the seams to close them well. Using the tip of your finger, wet the two diagonal sides and begin sealing the seam on the left side making small folds from the left side slightly over the right (similar to crimping a pie crust). Remember to line up the edges of the wrapper as you pleat and press all the way around. Continue pleating seven to ten times until the dumpling is completely sealed. The finished dumpling will have a half-moon shape. (See more on page 58.) Place the finished dumpling on a sheet pan and cover with a tea towel or damp paper towel to keep them moist while working. Continue making dumplings until you have used all the filling and wrappers.

Place a large sauté pan with a tight-fitting lid over medium–high heat. Add 1 to 2 tablespoons (15 to 30 ml) of the soybean oil to the pan and heat to a shimmer, 3 to 4 minutes. Add six to eight dumplings to the pan at a time to prevent crowding and cook for 4 to 5 minutes, until the bottoms of the dumplings are brown and crispy. Carefully pour ¼ cup (60 ml) of water into the pan and cover the pan with a lid. Let the dumplings steam for 3 to 4 minutes, until the filling is cooked through and the skin has formed a tight seal (the dumplings should lift easily from the bottom of the pan). Cook the rest of the dumplings in batches of six to eight, adding more oil as necessary.

Serve immediately with soy sauce for dipping.

Vegan Lovers Dumplings

These vegan lovers dumplings feature gluten-free wonton wrappers. These are also a good choice if someone can't tolerate tofu and is a vegan. Personally, I find that it's a lot more fun to include everyone in dumpling making, and I love when people play around with their food. You can have a dumpling party and make a variety of dumplings—totally vegan recipes mean everyone can participate. Plus, these are tasty!

2 tbsp (30 ml) coconut aminos, plus more for dipping

1 tsp fresh ginger, peeled and minced

2 cloves garlic, minced

2 tbsp (30 ml) rice wine vinegar

1 tbsp (8 g) cornstarch

5–8 tbsp (75–120 ml) soybean oil, divided

1 cup (70 g) white button or cremini mushrooms, chopped

1 cup (130 g) carrots, grated

2 cups (140 g) green cabbage, finely shredded

24 gluten-free wonton wrappers, rolled thin

Combine the coconut aminos, ginger, garlic, vinegar and cornstarch in a small bowl. Whisk to combine and set aside.

Place a nonstick skillet over medium–high heat and add 2 tablespoons (30 ml) of the soybean oil. Heat the oil until it starts to shimmer, then add the mushrooms, carrots and cabbage. Cook the mixture for 5 to 6 minutes, until the vegetables begin to wilt, then add about ⅓ cup (80 ml) of water, cover the pan, and let the veggies steam for 4 to 5 minutes over medium heat until soft. Remove the cover, add the sauce mixture, and stir until everything comes together and all additional water has evaporated, 1 to 2 minutes. Remove the filling from the heat and allow it to cool for 5 to 10 minutes.

Lay a wonton dough square on a clean work surface at an angle, so that it looks like a diamond. Place 1 heaping teaspoon of the veggie filling in the center of the wonton square. Wet your fingers in a small bowl of water and run a damp finger along all four outside edges of the wrapper.

Carefully pick up the wonton skin and lay it in the palm of your hand, keeping the points pointing up toward your middle finger and down to the base of your palm. Gently fold the bottom point of the skin up over the filling, creating a triangle, then gently press the seams to close them well. Using the tip of your finger, wet the two diagonal sides and begin sealing the seam on the left side making small folds from the left side slightly over the right (similar to crimping a pie crust). Remember to line up the edges of the wrapper as you pleat and press all the way around. Continue pleating seven to ten times until the dumpling is completely sealed. The finished dumpling will have a half-moon shape. (See more on page 58.) Place the finished dumpling on a sheet pan and cover with a tea towel or damp paper towel to keep them moist while working. Continue making dumplings until you have used all the filling and wrappers.

Place a large sauté pan with a tight-fitting lid over medium–high heat. Add 1 to 2 tablespoons (15 to 30 ml) of the soybean oil to the pan and heat to a shimmer, 3 to 4 minutes. Add six to eight dumplings to the pan at a time to prevent crowding and cook for 4 to 5 minutes, until the bottoms of the dumplings are brown and crispy. Carefully pour ¼ cup (60 ml) of water into the pan and cover the pan with a lid. Let the dumplings steam for 3 to 4 minutes, until the filling is cooked through and the skin has formed a tight seal (the dumplings should lift easily from the bottom of the pan). Cook the rest of the dumplings in batches of six to eight, adding more oil as necessary.

Serve immediately with coconut aminos for dipping.

Soup's On

Parlez Vous French Onion Soup Dumplings

YIELD: 24 DUMPLINGS

6 tbsp (84 g) unsalted butter

4 yellow onions, sliced thin

2 cloves garlic, minced

2 bay leaves

4 sprigs fresh thyme

1 cup (240 ml) dry red wine

1 tbsp (18 g) kosher salt

½ tsp black pepper

3¾ cups (900 ml) beef broth

2 tbsp (15 g) unflavored gelatin

24 circular wonton wrappers, rolled thick

1½ cups (168 g) shredded Swiss or Gruyère cheese

You know how French onion soup is a savory treat on a winter day? These dumplings are a take on French onion soup and are among the most popular in my restaurant—they are a Brooklyn Chop House specialty. I have yet to meet someone who doesn't enjoy these.

You don't need to buy super expensive wine for these dumplings; just buy stuff you like drinking, so you can sip and cook. This is a low-waste cookbook!

In a large sauté pan over low heat, melt the butter. When the butter has melted and stopped foaming, add the onions, garlic, bay leaves and thyme. Cook the onions, stirring occasionally, for 25 to 35 minutes, until the onions are deeply caramelized and soft. Remove the pan from the heat and add the red wine, scraping the bottom of the pan to deglaze it. Return the pan to the heat and simmer until the wine has been completely absorbed. Remove the bay leaves and thyme stems, season with salt and pepper, and let the onions cool completely.

In a 9 x 13-inch (23 x 33-cm) pan, combine the beef broth and gelatin and stir well to combine. Add the caramelized onions and mix again so that the onions are spread evenly across the pan. Cover the pan with plastic wrap and place it in the refrigerator overnight to let the mixture set up completely.

Remove the pan from the refrigerator and carefully cut the solidified French onion soup into 1-inch (3-cm) squares.

Lay the circular wonton wrappers on a clean work surface. Pressing with your fingers, thin the outer rim of each wrapper, making sure to leave a thicker area at least 1 inch (3 cm) in diameter in the center of the wrapper. This will help keep any soup from leaking out during steaming. To test whether the outer edges of the wrapper are thin enough, hold the wrapper up to the light. If you can see the shadow of your fingers through the edges, the wrapper is ready.

In the center of each prepared wonton wrapper, place 1 tablespoon (7 g) of the shredded Swiss or Gruyère then place a French onion gelatin square on top of the cheese. Pick up the wrapper and place it in the center of your palm. Using using your index finger and thumb, begin to pleat and pinch the rim of the dough together to form a closed satchel (similar to a beggar's purse). Make sure to pinch and twist the dough at the end to completely close your dumpling (see more on page 116). Place the finished dumplings on a parchment-lined sheet pan and cover the dumplings with a towel to keep from drying out. Repeat with the remaining wrappers and filling.

Place a steamer basket over a pot of simmering water. Place eight to ten dumplings in the basket and close the lid. Steam for 10 to 12 minutes, until the filling is cooked through and the skins are tightly formed around the filling. Remove the dumplings from the basket and let cool for 2 to 3 minutes before serving. Repeat with the rest of the dumplings.

Funky Chunky Vegetable Soup Dumplings

YIELD: 24 DUMPLINGS

These dumplings take the classic soup dumpling form but are filled with vegetable goodness. These are also vegetarian, and you can make a meal out of them. You can use the gluten-free wrappers, if you wish, but regular wrappers work better—and be sure to roll the gluten-free wrappers ¼ inch (6 mm) thick for this recipe if you are making them yourself, as all the soup dumplings need a slightly thicker wrap.

To a deep sauté pan with a lid, add ¼ cup (60 ml) of the vegetable stock and the carrots, mushrooms, corn, salt and pepper. Bring the mixture to a boil, then lower the heat. Let the mixture come to a simmer then cover the pan. Gently steam the vegetables for 8 to 10 minutes, until the carrots can be easily pierced with a knife. Remove the steamed vegetables to a pan, draining away any leftover broth. Add the crumbled tofu and fresh basil and toss to combine. Season to taste with salt and pepper and let cool.

In a 9 x 13–inch (23 x 33–cm) pan, stir together the gelatin and 3¾ cups (0.9 L) of the vegetable stock until the gelatin is completely dissolved. Add the cooked vegetable and tofu mixture and stir so that the vegetables are evenly distributed across the pan. Move the pan to the refrigerator and let it sit overnight to firm up.

When ready to assemble the dumplings, remove the pan from the refrigerator and carefully cut the gelatin into 1-inch (3-cm) squares.

Lay the circular wonton wrappers on a clean work surface. Pressing with your fingers, thin the outer rim of each wrapper, making sure to leave a thicker area at least 1 inch (3 cm) in diameter in the center of the wrapper. This will help keep any soup from leaking out during steaming. To test whether the outer edges of the wrapper are thin enough, hold the wrapper up to the light. If you can see the shadow of your fingers through the edges, the wrapper is ready.

In the center of each prepared wonton wrapper, place a vegetable gelatin square. Pick up the wrapper and place it in the center of your palm. Using your index finger and thumb begin to pleat and pinch the rim of the dough together to form a closed satchel (similar to a beggar's purse). Make sure to pinch and twist the dough at the end to completely close your dumpling (see more on page 116). Place the finished dumplings on a parchment-lined sheet pan and cover the dumplings with a towel to keep from drying out. Repeat with the remaining wrappers and filling.

Place a steamer basket over a pot of simmering water. Place eight to ten dumplings in the basket and close the lid. Steam for 10 to 12 minutes, until the filling is cooked through and the skins are tightly formed around the filling. Remove the dumplings from the basket and let cool for 2 to 3 minutes before serving. Repeat with the rest of the dumplings.

Serve with soy sauce for dipping.

4 cups (960 ml) vegetable stock, divided

3 carrots, peeled and cut into ⅛-inch (3-mm) cubes

6 oz (170 g) white button mushrooms, diced

½ cup (77 g) corn, fresh or thawed from frozen

1 tsp kosher salt, plus more to taste

¼ tsp black pepper, plus more to taste

1 (14-oz [397-g]) block extra-firm tofu, crumbled

¼ cup (10 g) fresh basil, chiffonade

2 tbsp (14 g) vegetarian or kosher gelatin

24 circular wonton wrappers, rolled thick (see Note)

Soy sauce, for dipping

Note: If you'd like, when you make the wrappers for this recipe you can use beet juice in place of the water. A word of warning though, when working with the beet juice wonton dough, you may want to wear food-safe gloves to prevent your hands from turning pink.

Decadent King Crab Soup Dumplings

YIELD: 24 DUMPLINGS

CRAB BOIL (SEE NOTE)

8 cups (1.92 L) water

5 scallions, ends removed, chopped into 3-inch (8-cm) pieces

2-inch (5-cm) piece fresh ginger, skin on, sliced thin

2–3 cloves garlic, crushed and paper removed

2–3 tbsp (30–45 ml) soy sauce

2–3 tbsp (30–45 ml) shaoxing wine (or rice wine vinegar)

5 lbs (2.27 kg) king crab legs, shell on

CRAB FILLING

3¾ cups (0.9 L) reserved crab boil broth

2 tbsp (14 g) unflavored gelatin

2 cups (448 g) shelled crabmeat

3 scallions, sliced thin

3 tbsp (45 ml) soy sauce

3 cloves garlic, minced

2 tbsp (12 g) fresh ginger, peeled and minced

2 tbsp (30 ml) sesame oil

2 tbsp (30 ml) rice wine vinegar

Salt and pepper, to taste

24 circular wonton wrappers, rolled thick

Soy sauce, for dipping

There is nothing, and I mean nothing, more impressive in the seafood realm than a giant king crab leg. The succulent meat is prized because it is the absolute ultimate in decadence. I remember being a kid and being taught how to clean and eat these babies. Wanna impress? This is the recipe to use. Shaoxing wine is my preference, but rice wine vinegar works as a substitute and is probably easier to find.

In a large deep pot, combine the water, scallions, ginger, garlic, soy sauce and wine. Bring to a boil, then lower the heat and let the mixture simmer for 15 to 20 minutes to create a mild-flavored broth. Add the crab legs and let them simmer for approximately 20 minutes, until the shells turn bright red. Remove the crab legs and let them cool. Set the broth aside to cool. When the crab legs are cool enough to handle, crack the shells and remove the meat to a bowl. Make sure to sift through the crabmeat and remove any pieces of shell and cartilage.

Place a colander or strainer over a large bowl and line it with a cheesecloth or paper towels. Carefully pour the cooled broth through the strainer to strain out the solids. Measure out 3¾ cups (0.9 L) of broth to use in your dumplings and save the rest for another use.

In a 9 x 13–inch (23 x 33–cm) pan, combine the reserved broth and the gelatin, stirring to completely dissolve the gelatin.

In a second bowl, combine the cleaned crabmeat, scallions, soy sauce, garlic, ginger, sesame oil and rice wine vinegar. Taste and season with salt and pepper if needed. Add the crabmeat mixture to the broth and combine so that the crab is evenly distributed across the pan. Let the pan sit in the refrigerator overnight to set up completely.

Remove the pan from the refrigerator and cut the gelatin mixture into 1-inch (3-cm) squares.

Lay the circular wonton wrappers on a clean work surface. Pressing with your fingers, thin the outer rim of each wrapper, making sure to leave a thicker area at least 1 inch (3 cm) wide in the center of the wrapper. This will help keep any soup from leaking out during steaming. To test whether the outer edges of the wrapper are thin enough, hold the wrapper up to the light. If you can see the shadow of your fingers through the edges, the wrapper is ready.

(continued)

Decadent King Crab Soup Dumplings (cont.)

Note: To save time, you may skip the crab boil step and simply purchase 2 cups (448 g) of shelled and cleaned crabmeat and 4 cups (960 ml) of fish or vegetable stock to use in the recipe.

In the center of each prepared wonton wrapper, place a crab gelatin square. Pick up the wrapper and place it in the center of your palm. Using your index finger and thumb, begin to pleat and pinch the rim of the dough together to form a closed satchel (similar to a beggar's purse). Make sure to pinch and twist the dough at the end to completely close your dumpling (see more on page 116). Place the finished dumplings on a parchment-lined sheet pan and cover the dumplings with a towel to keep from drying out. Repeat with the remaining wrappers and filling.

Place a steamer basket over a pot of simmering water. Place eight to ten dumplings in the basket and close the lid. Steam for 10 to 12 minutes, until the filling is cooked through and the skins are tightly formed around the filling. Remove the dumplings from the basket and let cool for 2 to 3 minutes before serving. Repeat with the rest of the dumplings.

Serve with soy sauce for dipping.

Diner-Style Cream of Mushroom Soup Dumplings

YIELD: 24 DUMPLINGS

4 tbsp (56 g) unsalted butter

1 lb (454 g) cremini or white button mushrooms, chopped

4–5 sprigs fresh thyme, leaves stripped

½ cup (80 g) onion, chopped

8 tbsp (64 g) all-purpose flour

1 tsp kosher salt

¼ tsp black pepper

3 cups (720 ml) chicken stock

1 cup (240 ml) half-and-half

24 circular wonton wrappers, rolled thick

My all-time favorite soup as a kid was Campbell's Cream of Mushroom soup. I made it myself, always adding some milk. It was total comfort food. As an adult, one of the first soups I learned to make was homemade cream of mushroom soup and it turns out it also makes a really good dumpling. These are awesome—way better than soup from a can!

Place a large sauté pan over medium–high heat. Add the butter and when it melts completely and has stopped foaming, add the chopped mushrooms and fresh thyme. Let the mushrooms cook, without stirring, for 10 to 12 minutes, until the liquid from the mushrooms has evaporated and they are beginning to brown. Add the onion and cook, stirring occasionally for another 8 to 10 minutes, until the onion is soft but not brown.

Sprinkle the flour over the mushrooms and onion, and stir to create a roux. Stir the roux and cook for 4 to 5 minutes until the raw flour is cooked out, but the roux is still light in color. Add the salt and pepper. Carefully pour in the chicken stock, stirring constantly to prevent any lumps from forming. Add the half and half and bring the mixture to a boil then lower the heat and simmer for 6 to 8 minutes, until the mixture has thickened. Remove the pan from the heat.

Pour the soup into a 9 x 13–inch (23 x 33–cm) pan and set the pan in the freezer for 3 to 4 hours. The soup should be partially frozen. Using a small, sharp knife, score the soup into 1-inch (3-cm) pieces, then place the pan back into the freezer for another 2 to 3 hours, or overnight.

Remove the soup from the freezer. Using a sharp knife, following the scoring lines you previously made, cut the soup into 1-inch (3-cm) pieces (they will not be perfectly square, but don't worry about it; as long as they are roughly that size they will be fine).

Line a sheet pan with parchment paper and set aside.

Lay the circular wonton wrappers on a clean work surface. Pressing with your fingers, thin the outer rim of each wrapper, making sure to leave a thicker area at least 1 inch (3 cm) in diameter in the center of the wrapper. This will help keep any soup from leaking out during steaming. To test whether the outer edges of the wrapper are thin enough, hold the wrapper up to the light. If you can see the shadow of your fingers through the edges, the wrapper is ready.

(continued)

Diner-Style Cream of Mushroom Soup Dumplings (cont.)

In the center of each prepared wonton wrapper, place a mushroom soup square. Pick up the wrapper and place it in the center of your palm. Using your index finger and thumb, begin to pleat and pinch the rim of the dough together to form a closed satchel (similar to a beggar's purse). Make sure to pinch and twist the dough at the end to completely close your dumpling (see more on page 116). Place the finished dumplings on the parchment-lined sheet pan and cover the dumplings with a towel to keep from drying out. Repeat with the remaining wrappers and filling.

Place a steamer basket over a pot of simmering water. Place eight to ten dumplings in the basket and close the lid. Steam for 10 to 12 minutes, until the filling is cooked through and the skins are tightly formed around the filling. Remove the dumplings from the basket and let cool for 2 to 3 minutes before serving. Repeat with the rest of the dumplings.

Mom's Classic Organic Chicken Soup Dumplings

I think of my mom when I have chicken soup, so I decided to make a dumpling based on one of my favorites. There's nothing better than homemade soup when you need a lift. I don't think chicken soup ever gets old!

In a large pot combine the water, onion, carrots, celery, bay leaves, peppercorns, oregano, parsley, lemons, salt and pepper. Bring the mixture to a boil then lower the heat to a simmer. Add the chicken thighs and cover the pot. Simmer the mixture for 45 to 60 minutes, until the chicken is falling off the bone. Remove the chicken from the pot and separate the meat from the skin and bones. Shred the chicken and set it aside (you will have approximately 1½–2 cups [210–280 g] of chicken).

Place a strainer over a large bowl and line it with a cheesecloth or paper towels. Carefully pour the stock through the strainer to remove all the solids. Reserve 3¾ cups (0.9 L) of the stock to use now and save the rest for another use.

In a 9 x 13–inch (23 x 33–cm) pan, combine the reserved chicken stock with the gelatin, stirring well to dissolve the gelatin. Add the shredded chicken to the pan and combine so that the chicken is evenly distributed across the pan. Set the pan in the refrigerator overnight to set up.

Remove the pan from the refrigerator and cut the gelatin into 1-inch (3-cm) squares.

Line a sheet pan with parchment paper and set aside.

Lay the circular wonton wrappers on a clean work surface. Pressing with your fingers, thin the outer rim of each wrapper, making sure to leave a thicker area at least 1 inch (3 cm) in diameter in the center of the wrapper. This will help keep any soup from leaking out during steaming. To test whether the outer edges of the wrapper are thin enough, hold the wrapper up to the light. If you can see the shadow of your fingers through the edges, the wrapper is ready.

In the center of each prepared wonton wrapper, place a chicken gelatin square. Pick up the wrapper and place it in the center of your palm. Using your index finger and thumb, begin to pleat and pinch the rim of the dough together to form a closed satchel (similar to a beggar's purse). Make sure to pinch and twist the dough at the end to completely close your dumpling. Place the finished dumplings on the parchment-lined sheet pan and cover the dumplings with a towel to keep from drying out. Repeat with the remaining wrappers and filling.

Place a steamer basket over a pot of simmering water. Place eight to ten dumplings in the basket and close the lid. Steam for 10 to 12 minutes, until the filling is cooked through and the skins are tightly formed around the filling. Remove the dumplings from the basket and let cool for 2 to 3 minutes before serving. Repeat with the rest of the dumplings.

YIELD: 24 DUMPLINGS

8 cups (1.9 L) water

1 onion, skin on, cut into quarters

2 carrots, chopped into 2-inch (5-cm) pieces

2 stalks celery, chopped into 2-inch (5-cm) pieces

2 bay leaves

5–6 whole peppercorns

1 small bunch fresh oregano

1 bunch parsley

2 lemons, halved

2 tbsp (30 g) kosher salt

1 tbsp (8 g) black pepper

2 lbs (908 g) chicken thighs, bone in, skin on

2 tbsp (14 g) unflavored gelatin

24 circular wonton wrappers, rolled thick

Perfect Pork Soup Dumplings

YIELD: 24 DUMPLINGS

⅔ cup (160 ml) hot water

1 tbsp (7 g) unflavored gelatin

1 tbsp (15 ml) soy sauce

1 tbsp (15 ml) chicken stock

1 lb (454 g) ground pork

3 scallions, finely chopped

4 oz (113 g) shiitake mushrooms, stems removed and finely chopped

1 (½-inch [13-mm]) piece fresh ginger, peeled and grated

2 cloves garlic, grated

2 tsp (10 ml) sesame oil

1 tsp sake

24 circular wonton wrappers, rolled thick

I love ramen. It's really hard to do well, but when you eat some good ramen . . . you know it. These Perfect Pork Soup Dumplings are a riff on ramen, and the delicate seasonings really make these delicious. You can find sake in any liquor store, and it really brings out the flavor of the broth. These are completely slurpworthy. (Which, by the way, is polite—slurping is a way of saying "this is good!")

Add the hot water, gelatin, soy sauce and chicken stock to a medium bowl. Stir to combine. Pour the mixture into a 5 x 7–inch (13 x 18–cm) dish and place the pan in the refrigerator for 1 hour, until set.

When set, fluff and break up the jellied soup with a fork.

In a medium bowl, combine the ground pork, scallions, mushrooms, ginger, garlic, sesame oil and sake. Mix with your hands until well combined.

Line a sheet pan with parchment paper and set aside.

Lay the circular wonton wrappers on a clean work surface. Pressing with your fingers, thin the outer rim of each wrapper, making sure to leave a thicker area at least 1 inch (3 cm) in diameter in the center of the wrapper. This will help keep any soup from leaking out during steaming. To test whether the outer edges of the wrapper are thin enough, hold the wrapper up to the light. If you can see the shadow of your fingers through the edges, the wrapper is ready.

In the center of each prepared wonton wrapper, place 1 tablespoon (15 g) of the pork filling, then add a spoonful of the jellied soup on top. Pick up the wrapper and place it in the center of your palm. Using your index finger and thumb, begin to pleat and pinch the rim of the dough together to form a closed satchel (similar to a beggar's purse). Make sure to pinch and twist the dough at the end to completely close your dumpling (see more on page 116). Place the finished dumplings on the parchment-lined sheet pan and cover the dumplings with a towel to keep from drying out. Repeat with the remaining wrappers and filling.

Place a steamer basket over a pot of simmering water. Place eight to ten dumplings in the basket and close the lid. Steam for 10 to 12 minutes, until the filling is cooked through and the skins are tightly formed around the filling. Remove the dumplings from the basket and let cool for 2 to 3 minutes before serving. Repeat with the rest of the dumplings.

Dessert Dumplings

American Dream Apple Wontons

YIELD: 24 DUMPLINGS

4 tbsp (56 g) unsalted butter

4 Granny Smith apples, peeled, cored and diced into ¼-inch (6-mm) pieces

¾ cup (165 g) brown sugar

1 tsp ground cinnamon

¼ tsp ground allspice

¼ tsp ground nutmeg

¼ cup (28 g) walnuts, chopped (optional)

24 wonton wrappers, rolled thin

1 cup (240 ml) soybean oil

Confectioners' sugar, for serving

Vanilla ice cream, for serving

Apple pie has been around even longer than America has been. Although apple pie and apple dumplings are a grand old tradition, the spices come from far and wide. The Brits love to spice fruit, and the recipes have trickled down in different incarnations as long as Brits have been here in America. In a sense, it is an immigrant recipe—although we consider apple pie as an all-American dessert. This apple pie dumpling is a sturdy, tasty version with apples wrapped in dough. You can serve these on July 4th, or any other day of the year.

In a medium saucepan over medium–high heat, melt the butter. When the butter has melted and stopped foaming, add the apples, brown sugar, cinnamon, allspice, nutmeg and walnuts, if using. Cook, stirring occasionally, for 10 to 12 minutes, until the apples are soft but still holding their shape. Remove the pan from the heat and let the apple mixture cool.

Fill a small bowl with water and set aside.

Lay out a wonton square with the points pointing up and down. Place 1 tablespoon (15 g) of the apple filling in the center of the square. Dip your fingers in the small bowl of water and using a damp finger, wet down the outside edges of the wrapper and lift it into the palm of your hand. Fold the bottom point up to the top and seal the wonton, pressing out the excess air. You should now have a triangle. Place the finished dumpling on a sheet pan and cover with a tea towel or damp paper towel to keep them moist while working. Continue making dumplings until you have used all the filling and wrappers.

Place a deep, heavy pan over medium–high heat, add the oil and heat until the oil begins to shimmer. Carefully place six to eight wontons into the hot oil (frying too many wontons at once will lower the temperature of the oil too fast, and your wontons will be greasy instead of crispy). Let the dumplings fry for 4 to 5 minutes on each side, until lightly browned and crispy. Drain on paper towels.

Serve immediately dusted with confectioners' sugar alongside vanilla ice cream.

Fried Banana Dumplings

These banana dumplings are a takeoff on the fried banana desserts you used to get at Chinese restaurants. They are really good with vanilla ice cream, but just as good plain. Cardamom adds a little something special, and the fried dough balls are addictive. Sprinkle on confectioners' sugar at the end, just before serving, and make sure they don't sit—these are best straight to the table.

In a large bowl, mash the bananas well with a wooden spoon or potato masher. Gently fold in the whole-wheat flour, cardamom, confectioners' sugar, baking powder and salt to create a fairly thick batter. Let the batter rest for 20 minutes.

In a deep pan, heat the oil to 365°F (185°C). Using a melon baller or small cookie scoop, form 2-inch (5-cm) balls of batter, rolling the balls in your hands to smooth away any rough edges. Gently lower four to six balls of batter at a time into the hot oil and fry for 4 to 6 minutes, rolling gently if needed, until the balls are golden brown. Drain the balls on paper towels and repeat with the rest of the batter.

Serve immediately garnished with extra confectioners' sugar.

YIELD: 24 DUMPLINGS

4 ripe bananas (mostly brown)

2 cups (240 g) whole-wheat flour

¾ tsp ground green cardamom

½ cup (60 g) confectioners' sugar, plus extra for garnish

2 tsp (8 g) baking powder

¼ tsp kosher salt

2 cups (480 ml) soybean oil

Dark Melted Chocolate Dumplings

YIELD: 24 DUMPLINGS

DUMPLINGS

2½ cups (315 g) all-purpose flour

4 tsp (16 g) baking powder

1 tsp kosher salt

1 cup (200 g) sugar

4 tbsp (22 g) cocoa powder

6 tbsp (84 g) unsalted butter, cold, cut into pieces

2 large eggs, lightly beaten

⅔ cup (160 ml) whole milk (you can substitute 2% milk, but anything less will not create the correct consistency)

2 tsp (10 ml) vanilla extract

CHOCOLATE SAUCE

1½ cups (330 g) brown sugar, packed

½ cup (43 g) cocoa powder

2 tbsp (16 g) cornstarch

¼ tsp kosher salt

3 cups (720 ml) water

4 tbsp (56 g) unsalted butter, sliced into pats

Whipped cream or vanilla ice cream, for serving

Chocolate on chocolate tends to be a huge hit, and these Dark Melted Chocolate Dumplings harken back to the classic molten chocolate cake. The chocolate dumplings float in a rich chocolate sauce, just oozing everywhere. The end result is worth it, and you can serve it with vanilla ice cream or whipped cream to "sweeten" the deal. Valentine's Day, perhaps?

To make the dumplings, in a large bowl, sift together the flour, baking powder, salt, sugar and cocoa powder. Using a pastry cutter, two knives or clean fingers, add the cold butter to the bowl and cut the butter into the flour mixture until it resembles a coarse meal. In a separate bowl, combine the eggs, milk and vanilla. Using a fork, slowly work the liquids into the dry mixture, stirring until just combined. Form the dough into 2-inch (5-cm) balls and set aside on a sheet pan.

To make the chocolate sauce, in a large, deep saucepan over medium heat, combine the brown sugar, cocoa powder, cornstarch and salt. Slowly add the water, stirring constantly, until the sauce begins to thicken. Add the butter a couple of pats at a time, then bring the sauce to a simmer. Gently drop the dumplings into the sauce and cover the pan. Cook gently for approximately 20 minutes, until the dumplings are just set. Serve immediately with whipped cream or vanilla ice cream.

Five-Spice Caramel Apple Cinnamon Sugar Dumplings

A few years ago, I found a friend's grandmother's 100-year-old spiced apple pie recipe. I was excited to put my spin on it and add the classic five-spice blend to a dumpling. The addition of cream acts almost as a custard. This dessert dumpling would be great for holidays, especially served with the Sweet Potato Pie Dumplings (page 142) because the spice would match up well with the maple syrup in that recipe. Make sure to serve these dumplings with the caramel sauce—it makes this dessert extra special.

YIELD: 24 DUMPLINGS

Juice of 1 lemon

1 tbsp (8 g) cornstarch

3–4 Granny Smith apples, peeled and diced into ¼-inch (6-mm) cubes

¼ cup (55 g) light brown sugar, packed

¼ cup + 2 tbsp (76 g) granulated sugar, divided

1 tsp five-spice powder

⅛ tsp kosher salt

⅛ tsp vanilla extract

2 tbsp (30 ml) heavy cream

4 tbsp (56 g) unsalted butter

2 tbsp (16 g) cinnamon

24 wonton wrappers, rolled thick

3 cups (720 ml) soybean oil

Vanilla ice cream, for serving

Caramel sauce, for serving

Confectioners' sugar, for garnish

In a large bowl, combine the lemon juice and cornstarch, whisking well to combine. Add the apples, brown sugar and ¼ cup (50 g) of granulated sugar, five-spice powder, salt, vanilla and heavy cream and toss to combine.

In a large sauté pan, melt the butter over medium–high heat, add the apple mixture and cook for 8 to 10 minutes, stirring occasionally, until the apples are softened and beginning to caramelize. Remove the pan from the heat and let the apple mixture cool completely.

In a small bowl, combine the cinnamon and 2 tablespoons (26 g) of the granulated sugar and set aside.

Lay a wonton dough square on a clean work surface at an angle, so that it looks like a diamond. Place 1 heaping tablespoon (15 g) of the apple mixture in the middle of the wrapper. Dip your fingers in a small bowl of water and using a damp finger, wet down the outside edges of the wrapper and lift it into the palm of your hand. Fold the bottom point up to the top and seal the wonton, pressing out the excess air. You should now have a triangle. Wet the bottom points and fold them in on each other to create a tortellini-shaped wonton (see more on page 54).

Place a large, deep pot over medium–high heat. Add the soybean oil and heat to 365°F (185°C). Carefully drop five to six wontons at a time into the hot oil and fry for 4 to 5 minutes, until lightly browned. Remove the wontons from the oil and drain briefly on paper towels. Transfer the drained but still hot wontons into the sugar and cinnamon mixture and toss to coat. Serve immediately with ice cream, caramel sauce and confectioners' sugar.

Warm Berries 'n' Dumplings

1 lb (454 g) frozen mixed berries

2 tbsp (30 ml) lemon juice

7 tbsp (105 g) sugar, divided

1 cup (125 g) all-purpose flour

2 tsp (8 g) baking powder

1 tsp baking soda

¼ tsp kosher salt

4 tbsp (56 g) unsalted butter, cold and cubed

1 cup (240 ml) buttermilk, cold

¼ tsp cinnamon

Vanilla ice cream, for serving (optional)

There is a whole world of regional fruit dumplings. This recipe uses berries, but you can substitute any fruit in the same proportions. These are home cooking at its finest. If you like a crumble or slump, this will be your favorite fruit dessert in the dumpling family. The fruit cooks down and turns into a compote, and the dough is warm and filling. This can also be served at brunch. If you like, you can add a scoop of vanilla ice cream.

In a cast-iron skillet, or a deep, heavy skillet with a tight-fitting lid, combine the berries, lemon juice, 4 tablespoons (60 g) of the sugar, and ¼ cup (60 ml) of water. Stir the mixture well and cook over medium–high heat for 12 to 15 minutes, until the berries are beginning to break down and the mixture has thickened slightly.

While the fruit is cooking, in a large bowl combine the flour, 2 tablespoons (30 g) of the sugar, the baking powder, baking soda and salt to combine. Add the cold butter and, using a pastry cutter or two forks, cut the butter into the flour mixture until it resembles coarse meal. Slowly stir in the buttermilk until just combined. Divide the dough into six equal pieces and drop them onto the berry mixture in the pan. Sprinkle the dumplings with the cinnamon and the remaining tablespoon (15 g) of sugar.

Cover the pan with the lid (or with foil), and adjust the heat to medium. Cook for 15 to 20 minutes, until the dumplings are just cooked through and dry to the touch. Serve warm, scooped into bowls topped with ice cream, if using.

Old-School Maple Dumplings

Maple syrup is a classic North American staple, and these dumplings are a delicious way to enjoy the flavor. It is a seasonal delicacy, and often enjoyed in the winter, but we are lucky enough now to be able to just get it at the grocery store.

This dumpling is not just great as a dessert; it can also be enjoyed at brunch. Make sure you don't crowd the pan with dough as you cook—that can lower the temperature, which will make the dough "flat," or spongy.

Line a sheet pan with parchment paper.

In a large bowl, stir together the flour, baking powder, cinnamon and salt until well combined. Add the cubed butter and using a pastry cutter or two forks, cut the butter into the flour mixture until pea-sized pieces of butter remain. Using a fork, stir in the milk until the batter forms a loose mass, similar to a bread dough. Dust your hands with flour and then form 2-inch (5-cm) balls of dough. Set the rolled balls on the parchment-lined sheet pan and cover them with a towel.

Combine the maple syrup and water in a deep sauté pan over medium heat and bring the mixture to a simmer. Add the balls of dough to the maple mixture and simmer until cooked through, about 20 minutes. You may need to work in batches.

Serve hot with vanilla ice cream.

YIELD: 12–15 DUMPLINGS

2½ cups (315 g) all-purpose flour, plus extra for dusting your hands

2 tbsp (24 g) baking powder

1 tsp cinnamon

¼ tsp kosher salt

6 tbsp (84 g) unsalted butter, cold, cubed

1 cup (240 ml) whole milk

2 cups (480 ml) maple syrup

1½ cups (360 ml) water

Vanilla ice cream, for serving

Cinnamon Saffron Dumplings

YIELD: 16 DUMPLINGS

2 cups (250 g) all-purpose flour

2 tsp (8 g) baking powder

1 cup (230 g) marzipan, room temperature

3 cups (720 ml) whole milk

1 tsp vanilla extract

1 tsp cinnamon

½ tsp ground nutmeg

¼ tsp saffron threads

Saffron is a spice from the Middle East that has a very subtle, almost honey quality. Its flavor is hard to pin down—it is delicate but adds depth and sweetness. You know saffron when you taste it, but it doesn't taste like anything else. It is luxurious. Here we use it to create a dumpling that has warmth and can be served when it's cold outside. The marzipan is perfect for traditional holiday menus. This dumpling almost tastes like a macaron.

Line a sheet pan with parchment paper. In a large bowl, combine the flour, baking powder and marzipan until it forms a stiff paste. Cut the paste into chunks the size of the end of your thumb and roll the chunks into balls. Place the balls on the parchment-lined sheet pan and cover them with a towel.

In a large pot over medium heat, combine the milk, vanilla, cinnamon, nutmeg and saffron threads. Bring the mixture to a simmer, being careful not to boil, as the milk will curdle.

Gently drop the dumplings into the simmering milk and cook gently at a simmer for 12 to 15 minutes. The dumplings will rise to the top of the pot when they are ready.

To serve, place the dumplings into a bowl and pour some of the cooking liquid over the top.

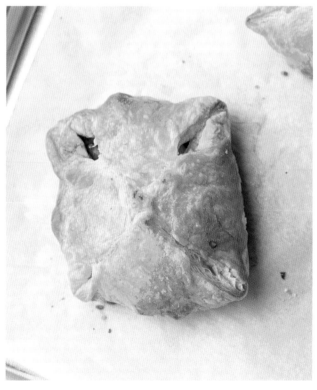

Pear Dumplings

Dumplings come in several forms, and the American way is to wrap fruit in dough, cooking until the pastry is brown and the fruit is tender. These dumplings use pears, which are delightful in season. I prefer them to apples. The ginger in this recipe adds a little heat and the orange ginger sauce really elevates these dumplings. Feel free to omit the nuts if there is an allergy in the house.

Preheat the oven to 375°F (190°C). Line a sheet pan with parchment paper; set aside.

Lightly flour a work surface. Lay the puff pastry sheet on the work surface and gently roll it out until it is ⅛ to ¼ inch (3 to 6 mm) thick. Using a sharp knife, cut the pastry in half lengthwise, and then cut each strip into three equal pieces. Sprinkle the dough with the brown sugar and cinnamon. Sprinkle the chopped pecans evenly across the six pieces of dough.

Lay a pear half, cut-side down, on each piece of puff pastry dough. Depending on the size of your pears, you may need to lay the pears at a diagonal (don't worry, the puff pastry is very forgiving and will stretch around your pears). Dot ¼ cup (56 g) of the butter cubes over the pears.

Using a pastry brush or your fingers, wet all four edges of the puff pastry with the beaten egg. Carefully fold all four sides of the puff pastry up around the pear, enclosing it like a package. Pinch the seams to ensure proper seals. Using the remaining egg wash, brush all of the packages lightly. Place the pear packages onto the prepared sheet pan and place it in the oven. Bake for 25 minutes.

While the pear packets are baking, prepare the sauce. In a medium saucepan, combine the water, sugar, orange rind and ginger. Bring to a boil, then drop to a simmer. Cook for 6 to 8 minutes, until all of the sugar has dissolved and the syrup reduces slightly. Remove the pan from the heat and pour the syrup through a strainer into a clean bowl. Gently swirl in 1 tablespoon (14 g) of the butter and whisk to incorporate; the syrup should now have a silky texture.

Place the pear packets on a platter and pour the orange ginger syrup over the top to serve.

YIELD: 6 DUMPLINGS

2–3 tbsp (24 g) all-purpose flour for dusting

1 sheet puff pastry, thawed

¼ cup (55 g) packed brown sugar

1 tsp ground cinnamon

½ cup (55 g) chopped pecans

3 pears, peeled, stem removed and cut in half from top to bottom, cored

¼ cup + 1 tbsp (70 g) unsalted butter, cubed, divided

1 egg, lightly beaten

1½ cups (360 ml) water

1½ cups (300 g) sugar

1 (2–3-inch [5–8-cm]) piece of orange rind

1 thin slice of fresh ginger

Ginger Apple Dumplings

YIELD: 16 DUMPLINGS

2 (8-oz [227-g]) packages of refrigerated crescent roll dough

3 Gala or Granny Smith apples, peeled, cored and cut into 6 wedges

12 tbsp (168 g) unsalted butter, plus extra for preparing the baking dish

1 cup (220 g) packed brown sugar

1 tsp vanilla extract

1 (12-oz [355-ml]) can ginger ale

Cinnamon, for dusting

Vanilla ice cream, for serving

These are a fun dumpling surprise, and every kid I know loves these. They consist of little packets of dough wrapped around an apple slice. A butter mixture is poured over the snug little apple slices, and the finishing touch is a can of ginger ale poured around the dough. The kids are impressed you can cook with soda, which makes these dumplings a little gooey. These are clever little treats, and are perfect at Thanksgiving to take the place of a traditional apple pie. These are also awesome for brunch.

Preheat the oven to 350°F (175°C). Butter a 9 x 13–inch (23 x 33–cm) baking dish.

Unroll the crescent dough and carefully separate each individual piece (you should have sixteen). Take one apple wedge and wrap it with one piece of crescent dough (you will have two apple slices left over—these are chef snacks!). Place the wrapped apples into the prepared baking dish so that the apples are on their sides. It will be a tight fit, but just snug them all in.

In a small saucepan, melt the butter over medium heat. Add the brown sugar and vanilla and cook, stirring, until the sugar is melted. Pour the butter–sugar mixture evenly over the apples. Pour the ginger ale around the sides and down the middle of the pan. Sprinkle the cinnamon over the top.

Bake the apple packets, uncovered, for 35 to 40 minutes, until the tops are brown and crispy. Serve with vanilla ice cream, as well as the sauce left over in the bottom of the pan.

PB&J Dumplings

These dumplings take the quintessential American classic, peanut butter and jelly, and makes a little dippy snack. The warm and melting peanut butter melds with the jelly dipping sauce and combines to make a total winner. These are nostalgia with a twist. You can use any jelly or jam you like, whether it's grape, raspberry or strawberry. Personally, I like grape—the lunch box classic.

YIELD: 24 DUMPLINGS

24 wonton wrappers, rolled thin

24 tbsp (384 g) creamy peanut butter (I prefer Skippy)

3 tbsp (42 g) unsalted butter, divided

Fruit jam or jelly of choice, for dipping

Fill a small bowl with water and set aside.

Lay a wonton dough square on a clean work surface at an angle, so that it looks like a diamond. Place 1 heaping teaspoon of peanut butter in the center of the wonton square. Wet your fingers in the small bowl of water and run a damp finger along all four outside edges of the wrapper.

Carefully pick up the wonton skin and lay it in the palm of your hand, keeping the points pointing up toward your middle finger and down to the base of your palm. Gently fold the bottom point of the skin up over the filling, creating a triangle, then gently press the seams to close them well. Using the tip of your finger, wet the two diagonal sides and begin sealing the seam on the left side making small folds from the left side slightly over the right (similar to crimping a pie crust). Remember to line up the edges of the wrapper as you pleat and press all the way around. Continue pleating seven to ten times until the dumpling is completely sealed. The finished dumpling will have a half-moon shape. (See more on page 58.) Place the finished dumpling on a sheet pan and cover with a tea towel or damp paper towel to keep them moist while working. Continue making dumplings until you have used all the filling and wrappers.

In a large sauté pan over medium heat, melt 1 tablespoon (14 g) of the butter. When the butter has melted and stopped foaming, lay eight wontons in the pan and cook for 4 to 5 minutes on each side. Remove the dumplings from the pan and let rest on a serving platter. Repeat this process with the remaining dumplings adding more butter for each batch as needed. Serve with the jam or jelly of your choice.

Sweet Potato Pie Dumplings

YIELD: 24 DUMPLINGS

2 medium sweet potatoes (about 1½ lbs [680 g]), peeled and cut into ½-inch (13-mm) cubes

⅓ cup (75 g) unsalted butter, softened

½ cup (100 g) sugar

2 large eggs, room temperature, lightly beaten

¾ cup (180 ml) evaporated milk

1 tsp vanilla extract

½ tsp ground cinnamon

½ tsp ground nutmeg

¼ tsp kosher salt

24 wonton wrappers, rolled thick

1 cup (240 ml) maple syrup, plus more for serving

1 cup (110 g) walnuts, roughly chopped

1 cup (240 ml) soybean oil

The South is known for desserts that are mouthwatering and filled with soul. A good sweet potato pie recipe is handed down from generation to generation. Sweet potato pie is actually served in place of pumpkin pie at Thanksgiving and Christmas in many places in the South. It has a warm mix of flavors and melts in your mouth. Maple syrup adds depth and is an unexpected element with the spices. The walnuts add crunch (of course, you can omit them, but they are really good—they add some festive flair).

Place the sweet potatoes in a medium saucepan with enough water to cover them over high heat. Bring the water to a boil, then reduce the heat to medium and cook, uncovered, until the sweet potatoes are tender, 13 to 15 minutes. Drain the potatoes and return them to the pan. Mash the sweet potatoes until they are very smooth and let them cool to room temperature.

In a medium bowl, cream the butter and sugar with a hand mixer. Add the eggs and mix well. Add the evaporated milk, 2 cups (500 g) of the mashed sweet potatoes, the vanilla, cinnamon, nutmeg and salt and mix well.

Lay a wonton dough square on a clean work surface at an angle, so that it looks like a diamond. Place 1 heaping teaspoon of the sweet potato filling in the center of the wonton square. Wet your fingers in a small bowl of water and run a damp finger along all four outside edges of the wrapper.

Carefully pick up the wonton skin and lay it in the palm of your hand, keeping the points pointing up toward your middle finger and down to the base of your palm. Gently fold the bottom point of the skin up over the filling, creating a triangle, then gently press the seams to close them well. Using the tip of your finger, wet the two diagonal sides and begin sealing the seam on the left side making small folds from the left side slightly over the right (similar to crimping a pie crust). Remember to line up the edges of the wrapper as you pleat and press all the way around. Continue pleating seven to ten times until the dumpling is completely sealed. The finished dumpling will have a half-moon shape. (See more on page 58.) Place the finished dumpling on a sheet pan and cover with a tea towel or damp paper towel to keep them moist while working. Continue making dumplings until you have used all the filling and wrappers.

In a small saucepan, combine the maple syrup and chopped walnuts over medium-high heat. Bring the mixture to a boil, then drop the heat to medium and let the mixture simmer for 6 to 8 minutes, until the walnuts become shiny and candied. Keep them warm while you complete the rest of the recipe.

Place a large, deep sauté pan over medium-high heat. Add the oil and heat it until it begins to shimmer. Place six to eight wontons at a time into the hot oil and fry for 4 to 5 minutes on each side, until lightly browned. Drain the dumplings on paper towels. Repeat with the remaining dumplings.

Serve immediately, drizzled with the candied walnuts and extra maple syrup.

Acknowledgments

Thank you to my late father, John N. Morfogen, and my mother, Beatrice Morfogen, for showing me the way and never giving up on me. To my three amazing daughters, Natalie, Beatriz and Isabel, for teaching me how to be the best father I can be. To my wife, Filipa Fino, who puts up with me and continues to be my strength and my heart. To "Cousin" Niki Maroulakos for always being there for me and my family unconditionally.

To my partners Robert "Don Pooh" Cummins and David Thomas for sharing this incredible culinary journey with me. To Jorge Mejia for being a great friend. To my chef Skinny Mei for always delivering on my culinary vision by keeping my "Who Said You Can't?" mindset alive.

To my most amazing culinary crew who made sure every recipe was perfect so my readers could enjoy the perfect dumpling experience at home! I couldn't have written this book without consulting Chef Nicolle Walker and Culinary Editor Jessa Moore.

To the great creative minds at Page Street Publishing, especially Marissa Giambelluca, Will Kiester and Meg Baskis for allowing me to express myself in the truest form I know and for allowing me to go outside the "norm" of traditional recipe books.

Damn Good Dumplings could not have been completed without such a high level of talent who passionately gave their all in bringing this special culinary work of art to life! This took much more than "a village" to publish; it took "my village."

Thank you to everyone—I am forever grateful!

About the Author

Stratis Morfogen is a well-known restaurateur in New York City. He is the owner of Brooklyn Chop House, which has been named "Best New Restaurant" by Thrillist and "Best Steakhouse in New York City" by *Newsweek*. Brooklyn Chop House has also been featured by *Forbes*, *Eater New York* and the *New York Post*, among others.

Stratis was also the founder of Philippe Chow and is a partner/owner of several establishments, including Jue Lan Club, Club Rouge, Gotham City Diner, The Grand, Pappas (forthcoming 2021) and others. Stratis has also partnered with Patti Labelle to sell his frozen dumplings in supermarkets across the country.

Upon completing this book, Stratis has expanded his vision of reinventing the dumpling to Main Street with Brooklyn Dumpling Shop, a culinary boutique franchise concept, bringing 32 flavors of delicious dumplings, 24 hours a day, nationwide. This QSR (Quick Service Restaurant) uses technological innovation inspired by the 19th century Automat to meet today's word health challenges providing a unique ZHI (Zero Human Interaction) fast-dining experience. He lives in New York City.

Index

149